Framework
English

Colin Thompson   Tim Woolstencroft

JN126073

KINSEIDO

Kinseido Publishing Co., Ltd.
3-21 Kanda Jimbo-cho, Chiyoda-ku,
Tokyo 101-0051, Japan
Copyright © 2020 by   Colin Thompson
                        Tim Woolstencroft

First published 2020 by Kinseido Publishing Co., Ltd.

Cover design   Nampoosha Co., Ltd.
Text design & editorial support   C-leps Co., Ltd.
Illustration   Hayato Kamoshita

Acknowledgements

The authors would like to thank the students, teachers and staff at Josai International University for their help during the writing and piloting of *Framework English*. In particular, we would like to thank President of JIU, Dr. Kenji Sugibayashi, and Vice-president of JIU, Masato Kurabayashi, for their continued support of this project.

A huge debt of thanks is owed to Professor Maria Shiguemi Ichiyama, Director of the Center for Language Education at JIU, for her invaluable advice and support. Thanks also to Yasuhiro Omoto for his great help.

Finally, we would like to express our sincerest thanks to Yukiko Thompson and Nobuko Ito, who provided inspiration, cultural help and language support, not to mention unstinting patience.

Additional acknowledgements

Photographs: Dreamstime
Pelmeni photo p.22 – Milena Pivinskaya
Hoppers photo p.22 – Mideki Fernando
CEFR-J wordlist - The CEFR-J Wordlist Version 1.5. Compiled by Yukio Tono, Tokyo University of Foreign Studies. Retrieved from http://www.cefrj.org/download.html#cefrj_wordlist on 01/09/2019.
Character images p.102-103
・兵庫県マスコットキャラクター「はばたん」
・沖縄観光 PR 大使「花笠マハエ」© OCVB
・大分県応援団 "鳥"「めじろん」
・長野県 PR キャラクター「アルクマ」© 長野県アルクマ 18-0102
・あおもり観光マスコットキャラクター「いくべぇ®」© 青森県観光連盟
・けんみん文化祭ひろしまマスコットキャラクター「ブンカッキー」

音声ファイル無料ダウンロード

http://www.kinsei-do.co.jp/download/4107

この教科書で 🔽 DL 00 の表示がある箇所の音声は、上記 URL または QR コードにて無料でダウンロードできます。自習用音声としてご活用ください。

▶ PC からのダウンロードをお勧めします。スマートフォンなどでダウンロードされる場合は、**ダウンロード前に「解凍アプリ」をインストール**してください。
▶ URL は、**検索ボックスではなくアドレスバー (URL 表示欄)** に入力してください。
▶ お使いのネットワーク環境によっては、ダウンロードできない場合があります。

◉ CD 00　左記の表示がある箇所の音声は、教室用 CD (Class Audio CD) に収録されています。

Introduction

Welcome to *Framework English*. This English language textbook is designed to improve learners' communicative and cognitive skills. The book is based on the aims and assessment criteria of the Common European Framework of Reference for Languages (CEFR). CEFR's goal for language learning is to prime learners to perform in real-life situations. As a result, its assessment criteria, focusing on communication, have been categorized into different proficiency levels (A1-C2). This action-based book primarily targets A1-A2 levels in terms of grammar. The vocabulary has been selected from A1-B2 CEFR-J levels; a CEFR informed word list designed for Asian learners of English. The selected language has been allocated within 7 topic-based modules of personal and social relevance for learners, such as food and fashion. These modules are looked at from international viewpoints so learners can improve their understanding of multiculturalism, and also learn to express their opinions about different cultures.

Each module follows a systematic structure. Learners are provided with clear learning goals, followed by a progression of tasks and activities that allow learners to practice and develop specific skills. The final section of each module consists of a "project" in which learners are required to answer a research question by collecting and reporting on data using the key language features of the module. In doing so, learners develop important cognitive skills such as analyzing information, reasoning, inferring, and displaying data. Learners then complete "Can-do" statements that reflect the goals outlined at the start of the module, enabling them to assess their strengths and weaknesses.

The communicative and cognitive skills gained from using Framework English not only benefit students' English study, but are also applicable to other areas of academic study, as well as their future careers.

Contents

		Match & Scan	Speak	Vocabulary	Grammar	Listen	Communicate
Module 1 Introductions	Unit 1	Where are they from? Scanning for personal information P. 6-7	Asking and answering personal questions P. 8	Introduction vocabulary P. 9	Asking and answering questions in the present simple P. 10	Two students meet for the first time P. 11	Who am I? Asking and answering questions to complete information cards P. 12-13
Module 2 Food	Unit 3	Match the food with the country Scanning for food information P. 22-23	Reporting and describing food habits P. 24	Food vocabulary P. 25	Yes/No questions in the present simple with adverbs of frequency P. 26	A conversation between two students cooking dinner P. 27	What do students think? Answering questions in a food survey P. 28
Module 3 Fashion	Unit 5	Match the fashion designs with the decades Scanning for fashion information P. 38-39	Describing likes and dislikes P. 40	Fashion vocabulary P. 41	Expressing likes and dislikes Talking about things you are doing now in the present continuous P. 42	A conversation between two students about shopping P. 43	How well do you know your classmates? Asking and answering questions about fashion P. 44
Module 4 Health	Unit 7	Match the person with the lifestyle Scanning for health information P. 54-55	Giving health advice P. 56	Health vocabulary P. 57	Asking for/giving advice in the present simple: "should/shouldn't" "must/mustn't" "try to/don't" "How" questions P. 58	A conversation between two students about their studies P. 59	How healthy are you? Completing a health survey P. 60
Module 5 Travel	Unit 9	Name the famous places Scanning for travel information P. 70-71	Reporting on past vacations P. 72	Travel vocabulary P. 73	Asking and answering questions about trips in the past simple P. 74	A conversation between two office workers about a trip abroad P. 75	Travelopoly: Communication board game about travel P. 76
Module 6 Rules	Unit 11	Where would you see these signs? Scanning for information about rules P. 86-87	Explaining rules and making suggestions P. 88	Rules voccabulary P. 89	Explaining laws, rules and customs using modal verbs in the present and past simple P. 90	Listening to explanations and announcements about rules P. 91	Culture Quiz: Rules of the World P. 92-93
Module 7 Culture	Unit 13	Name the famous sightseeing places in Japan Scanning for information about culture P. 102-103	Making recommendations P. 104	Culture vocabulary P. 105	Asking/answering questions about the future, giving recommendations "If" + simple present + main clause P. 106	A conversation between students planning a trip in Japan P. 107	Connect 5: Communication game about culture P. 108-109

		Read	Write	Project	Crossword	Language Review	Self-check
Module 1 Introductions	Unit 2	Reading a student's self-introduction message	Writing skill: Writing main ideas with supporting details Writing a self-introduction message	What do you know about your classmates? Using pie charts	Introduction vocabulary review	Introduction language review	What have you learned from this module?
		P. 14-15	P. 16-17	P. 18-19	P. 20	P. 119	P. 120
Module 2 Food	Unit 4	Reading a menu Reading a restaurant review in a food blog	Writing skill: Descriptive paragraph writing Writing a restaurant review	What are the eating habits of your classmates? Using column charts	Food vocabulary review	Food language review	What have you learned from this module?
		P. 29-30	P. 31-33	P. 34-35	P. 36	P. 121	P. 122
Module 3 Fashion	Unit 6	Reading fashion opinions	Writing skill: Opinion paragraph writing Writing about clothes	Do male and female students have similar fashion interests? Using Likert scales & line charts	Fashion vocabulary review	Fashion language review	What have you learned from this module?
		P. 45-46	P. 47-49	P. 50-51	P. 52	P. 123	P. 124
Module 4 Health	Unit 8	Reading about health problems and a doctor's advice	Writing skill: Cause, effect and solution Writing health advice	Who has the healthier lifestyle? Using Radar/spider charts	Health vocabulary review	Health language review	What have you learned from this module?
		P. 61-62	P. 63-65	P. 66-67	P. 68	P. 125	P. 126
Module 5 Travel	Unit 10	Reading a postcard from Hawaii Reading a review of a trip to Dubai	Writing skill: Mind-mapping Writing about a trip	Where are popular places to take a trip in Japan? Using interviews	Travel vocabulary review	Travel language review	What have you learned from this module?
		P. 77-79	P. 80-82	P. 83	P. 84	P. 127	P. 128
Module 6 Rules	Unit 12	Reading about high school and university rules	Writing skill: Narrative paragraph writing Writing about the rules at your high school and university	What rules are important for a Japanese university? Using pie charts & column charts	Rules vocabulary review	Rules language review	What have you learned from this module?
		P. 94-95	P. 96-97	P. 98-99	P. 100	P. 129	P. 130
Module 7 Culture	Unit 14	Reading a tourism advertisement about Hokkaido	Writing skill: Persuasive writing Writing a tourism advertisement	What are Japan's best tourist attractions? Using interviews	Culture vocabulary review	Culture language review	What have you learned from this module?
		P. 110-111	P. 112-113	P. 114-115	P. 116	P. 131	P. 132

3

Outline

Using Framework English

1 Match

Introduces the topic and activates learners' L2 resources

2 Scan

Learners practice scanning for information

3 Speak

Learners practice communicative functions

4 Vocabulary

Learners study topic-based CEFR-J vocabulary and engage in meaning-based vocabulary activities
Vocabulary levels: A1 – A2 – B1 – B2 – + (No level)

5 Grammar

Highlights the key grammar features of each module with activities for learners to practice

6 Listen

Learners listen to different perspectives then practice giving their own opinions on a topic

7 Communicate

Learners practice their communication skills by completing activities that use target vocabulary

8 Read

Pre-reading activities to activate learners' topic knowledge
Learners then read a topic-based text and answer comprehension questions

9 Write

Learners develop different writing skills by engaging in vocabulary, grammar and skill-based exercises

10 Project

Using the key vocabulary and grammar points of each module, learners complete a communicative, research-based project

11 Crossword

Learners test their knowledge of the module vocabulary by completing a fun crossword

12 Language Review

Learners review the module vocabulary and grammar by completing a series of exercises

13 Self-check

Helps learners to evaluate their knowledge and skills learned from each module using CEFR related can-do descriptors

4

MODULE

1

INTRODUCTIONS

Can you scan for information from introductions?

Can you introduce yourself and ask personal questions?

Can you understand introduction vocabulary?

Can you ask "Wh" and Yes/No personal questions?

Can you understand people when they introduce themselves?

Can you ask and answer personal questions about other people?

Can you read and understand introduction messages?

Can you write an email introducing yourself?

Can you find out personal information about your classmates?

★ *Match the pictures with the cards below. Write the letter of the card in the space next to the picture above.*

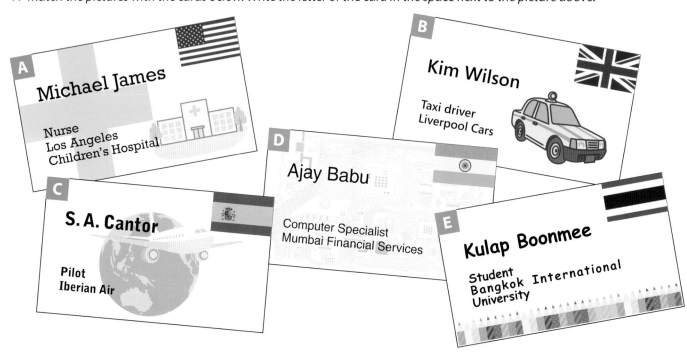

A
Michael James

Nurse
Los Angeles
Children's Hospital

B
Kim Wilson

Taxi driver
Liverpool Cars

C
S. A. Cantor

Pilot
Iberian Air

D
Ajay Babu

Computer Specialist
Mumbai Financial Services

E
Kulap Boonmee

Student
Bangkok International
University

SCAN: Where are they from?

A. Scanning for information: *In **4 minutes**, quickly read the information below to find key words.*

B. *Write the name of the country each person is from under the correct picture on page 6.* ⬇ DL 02 ◎ CD02

1.
My name is Michael, but all my friends call me Mike. I'm American. I'm from San Francisco, but I live and work in Los Angeles now. I love kids, and I work as a nurse in a children's hospital. In my free time, I enjoy watching sports. I'm a big fan of basketball.

2.

Nice to meet you. My name is Sofia Ana Cantor. My family name means singer in English. I'm Spanish, and I live in Madrid near the airport. I'm a pilot, and I love flying. I work for an airline in Spain. I think I have the best job in the world.

3.
I'm a taxi driver from Britain. In my free time, I love playing sport and watching movies. I especially like watching animation movies with my family. I live in Liverpool with my two young children, Oliver and Ella. Oh, I forgot to tell you my name, it's Kim Wilson. Nice to meet you.

4.

Hi, I'm Kulap. I'm from Thailand. I'm a student at a university in Bangkok. My major is Japanese, and I'm really interested in languages. As well as Thai, I also speak Chinese. In my free time, I'm really into reading Japanese manga and watching Japanese anime. My favorite is Naruto.

5.
I'm from Mumbai in India. I'm a computer specialist. I work for a large company. My name is Ajay. I love playing computer games in my free time, and I also like programming apps for my smart phone. I often stay up late and go online. I don't like getting up early. I'm not a morning person.

C. Introduce yourself: *Include your picture, your name, where you are from and what you do.*

SPEAK: Asking and answering personal questions

A. Introduction expressions: *Match the expressions with the pictures below.*

_____	I love watching soccer.	_____	I'm from California.
_____	I study Business.	_____	My name is John.
_____	I like listening to music and reading.	_____	I live in Kyoto.

B. Personal questions: *Match the questions below with the expressions above.*

_____	What's your name?	_____	Where are you from?
_____	What do you do for fun?	_____	Where do you live?
_____	What sports do you like?	_____	What's your major?

Think of an extra personal question and write it below:

_____

C. Let's talk! *In pairs, take turns asking the questions in part B and **giving your own answers**.*

For example:

A: *What's your name?*

B: *My name is Akira.*

A: *Where are you from?*

B: *I'm from Hokkaido.*

Bonus: Practice using different personal questions.

VOCABULARY

⬇ DL 03   ◉ CD03

Adjectives		brother ᴬ¹		student ᴬ¹	
favorite ᴬ¹	....	cooking ᴬ²	....	swimming ᴬ¹	....
interested ᴬ¹	....	country ᴬ²	....	university ᴬ²	....
old(er) ᴬ¹	....	culture ᴬ¹	....	**Verbs**	
online ᴬ¹	....	father ᴬ¹	....	be into ⁺	....
part-time ᴮ¹	....	free ᴬ¹ time ᴬ¹	....	graduate ᴬ²	....
young(er) ᴬ¹	....	friend ᴬ¹	....	hang out ⁺	....
Adverbs		(the) future ᴬ¹	....	listen ᴬ¹ (to music ᴬ¹)	....
late ᴬ¹	....	hobby ᴬ¹	....	play ᴬ¹	....
online ᴬ²	....	interest ᴬ²	....	(video games ᴬ²)	....
part-time ᴮ¹	....	job ᴬ¹	....	read ᴬ¹	....
really ᴬ¹	....	major ᴮ²	....	(comic ᴬ² books ᴬ¹)	....
well ᴬ¹	....	morning ᴬ¹ person ᴬ¹	....	stay up ⁺	....
Nouns		mother ᴬ¹	....	study ᴬ¹ (abroad ᴬ²)	....
baseball ᴬ¹	....	only ᴬ¹ child ᴬ¹	....	watch ᴬ¹ movies ᴬ¹	....
birthday ᴬ¹	....	parent ᴬ¹	....		
blood ᴬ² type ᴬ¹	....	sister ᴬ¹	....		

A. *Match each definition with the words on the right.*

1. A popular ball game in America: _____

2. Someone who studies at university: _____

3. Someone you like a lot: _____

4. To like something: _____

a) a student
b) a friend
c) be into
d) baseball

B. *Fill in the blanks using related words from the vocabulary list above.*

- mother _____
- _____ brother
- _____ child

C. Give your opinion!

1. I'm a morning person.
Agree: _____ Disagree: _____
Why? _____

2. I'm really into manga.
Agree: _____ Disagree: _____
Why? _____

3. I want to study abroad in the future.
Agree: _____ Disagree: _____
Why? _____

4. I like playing online video games.
Agree: _____ Disagree: _____
Why? _____

5. I like cooking in my free time.
Agree: _____ Disagree: _____
Why? _____

6. I want to live in Tokyo after I graduate.
Agree: _____ Disagree: _____
Why? _____

GRAMMAR

Asking and answering questions in the present simple

Present tense Wh- questions (Be verb)		Present tense Wh- questions (Other verbs)	
When is your birthday?	My birthday is June 2nd.	Where do you live?	I live in Fukuoka.
What's your major?	My major is Business.	Where does she live?	She lives in Madrid.
What country are you from?	I'm from Spain.	Where does he live?	He lives in Los Angeles.
Where are you from?	I'm from England.	Where do they live?	They live in Seoul.
Where is she from?	She's from China.	What music do you like?	I like J-pop.
Where is he from?	He's from Canada.	When do you study English?	I study English on Mondays and Wednesdays.
Where are they from?	They're from Russia.		
Yes/No questions (Be verb)		**Yes/No questions (Other verbs)**	
Is your birthday in May?	No, it isn't. It's in June.	Do you live in Kumamoto?	No, I don't. I live in Kagoshima.
Are you from India?	No, I'm not. I'm from Sri Lanka.	Does she live near here?	Yes, she does.
Is she from Japan?	Yes, she is. She's from Sendai.	Does he live in China?	Yes, he does. He lives in Dalian.
Is he from America?	Yes, he is. He's from Boston.	Do they live in Osaka?	No, they don't. They live in Kobe.
Are they from Italy?	No, they aren't. They're French.	Do you like J-pop?	Yes, I do. I like K-pop, too.

A. *Fill in the blanks and then match the questions with the answers.*

1. When _____ your birthday? _____
2. What _____ you do for fun? _____
3. _____ you from Chiba prefecture? _____
4. What _____ your blood type? _____
5. Where _____ your English teacher from? _____
6. _____ you live in Tokyo? _____
7. What _____ you do? _____
8. What kind of movies _____ you like? _____
9. _____ you play any sports? _____
10. _____ you interested in music? _____

a) I'm really into animation.
b) Yes, I am. I like all kinds of music. I play the piano.
c) No, I'm not. I'm from Akita prefecture.
d) I like hanging out with friends and going to karaoke.
e) Yes, I do. I live near Kita-Senju station in Adachi Ward.
f) I'm not sure, but I think she is from Canada.
g) My birthday is in May.
h) I'm a university student. My major is Business.
i) Yes, I do. I like soccer. I play twice a week.
j) It's AB.

★ *Now ask your partner the questions from part A.*

B. *Choose a, b, c or d.*

1. My birthday _____ January 2nd.
   a) is   b) are   c) do   d) does

2. Where is _____ English teacher from?
   a) you   b) your   c) a   d) has

3. I _____ from England.
   a) does   b) do   c) is   d) am

4. I _____ part-time at a convenience store.
   a) do   b) am   c) have   d) work

5. I live _____ Tokyo.
   a) is   b) in   c) a   d) the

LISTEN

A. Pre-listening

1. *Quickly read the conversation between two students meeting for the first time. Guess the missing words.*

2. *Listen to the conversation, check your answers and fill in the blanks.* 🎧 DL 04 ⊙ CD04

Hi, I'm Tom. What's _____ name?

Hi, my name is Min-Jun. Where _____ you from?

I'm from _____, but I _____ in Chiba now.

I'm from _____. I _____ to Japan last month.

I see. So, what's your _____?

English. Next year, I want to go abroad. I want to _____ in _____. How about you?

B. Discussion: *What do you think about this conversation?*

For example: "Next year, I want to go abroad." *I agree / don't agree with Min-Jun because ...*

C. *Listen to two more conversations between students. Choose the correct answer from a, b or c.*

Conversation 1 🎧 DL 05 ⊙ CD05

1. How often does Tom play soccer?
  a) Three times a day
  b) Three times a month
  c) Three times a week

2. What sport does Tom NOT play?
  a) Badminton   **b)** Basketball   **c)** Baseball

3. What days does Min-Jun NOT work?
  a) Wednesdays and Saturdays
  b) Tuesdays and Thursdays
  c) Tuesdays and Sundays

Conversation 2 🎧 DL 06 ⊙ CD06

1. How many brothers and sisters does Kota have?
  a) One older sister and one older brother.
  b) He's an only child.
  c) One older brother and one younger sister.

2. How often does Kota's brother return home?
  a) Twice a month   **c)** Three times a year
  b) Twice a year

3. What job does Kota's sister want?
  a) University teacher   **c)** Junior high school teacher
  b) High school teacher

D. Post-listening: *With a partner, continue the conversation between Tom and Min-Jun. Ask and answer more personal questions.*

COMMUNICATE: Who am I? (A)

A. *In pairs, student (A) looks at the cards on page 12, student (B) looks at the cards on page 13. Ask questions to find the missing information and fill in the cards.*
   Example: A (1A) - "What country is she from?" B (1A) - "She's from Norway."

B. *After you have filled out all the cards, complete your partner's card.*

1A

Name:
Country:
Home:
Job:
Birthday:
Interests:

1B

Name: Michel Blanc
Country: France
Home: Lyon
Job: Writer
Birthday: March 11
Interests: Playing the guitar

2A

Name: Siti Aziz
Country: Malaysia
Home: Kuala Lumpur
Job: Elementary school teacher
Birthday: August 2
Interests: Taking photographs

2B

Name:
Country:
Home:
Job:
Birthday:
Interests:

3A

Name:
Country:
Home:
Job:
Birthday:
Interests:

3B

Name: Martin Garcia
Country: Argentina
Home: Buenos Aires
Job: Retired
Birthday: July 21
Interests: Dancing (tango)

PARTNER

Name:
Country:
Home:
Job:
Birthday:
Interests:

COMMUNICATE: Who am I? (B)

A. *In pairs, student (A) looks at the cards on page 12, student (B) looks at the cards on page 13. Ask questions to find the missing information and fill in the cards.*
   Example: B (1B) - "What country is he from?" A (1B) - "He's from France."

B. *After you have filled out all the cards, complete your partner's card.*

1B

1A

Name:	Astrid Larsen
Country:	Norway
Home:	Oslo
Job:	Police officer
Birthday:	September 3
Interests:	Skiing

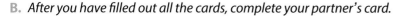

Name:
Country:
Home:
Job:
Birthday:
Interests:

2B

2A

Name:
Country:
Home:
Job:
Birthday:
Interests:

Name:	Seojun Choi
Country:	Korea
Home:	Incheon
Job:	Lawyer
Birthday:	December 20
Interests:	Shopping

3A

Name:	Zoe Campbell
Country:	Canada
Home:	Toronto
Job:	High school student
Birthday:	February 14
Interests:	Painting

Name:
Country:
Home:
Job:
Birthday:
Interests:

3B

PARTNER

Name:
Country:
Home:
Job:
Birthday:
Interests:

UNIT 2

READ

A. Brainstorm

First, think of three personal questions and answers.

For example: *name, hometown, interests*

B. Pre-reading

1. *Complete the questions below.*

2. *Look at the picture above, and try to guess the answers to the questions and write them down.*

3. *Quickly read the message on page 15 and check your answers.*

---

1. What _____ her name?

_____   _____
(Your answer)   (Correct answer)

2. Where _____ she from?

_____   _____
(Your answer)   (Correct answer)

3. Where _____ she live?

_____   _____
(Your answer)   (Correct answer)

4. What _____ she do?

_____   _____
(Your answer)   (Correct answer)

5. What sport _____ she like?

_____   _____
(Your answer)   (Correct answer)

6. What _____ she do for fun?

_____   _____
(Your answer)   (Correct answer)

C. *Read the student's self-introduction message. Answer the following questions.*

DL 07   CD07

Hi everyone,

My name's Andrea Smith. My friends call me Andi. I'm from Seattle, but I live in New York. I'm twenty years old, and I'm a student at a university there. I'm a Business major. I live in a small apartment near the university, and I work part-time in a fast food restaurant near my apartment.

My family lives in Seattle. My father is a businessman. He works for an IT company. My mother is a homemaker, and she also does volunteer work at a hospital in her free time. I have an older brother and a younger sister. My brother is studying Law in Los Angeles, and my sister is a high school student in Seattle.

In my free time, I'm into playing basketball and watching movies with my friends. I also like listening to music online and reading comic books. I love staying up late on weekends. I'm not a morning person!

Best,

Andi.

1. What does Andi study at university?
   a) Law
   b) IT
   c) Nursing
   d) Business

2. Where does Andi's father work?
   a) At a hospital
   b) At a police station
   c) At an information technology company
   d) At home

3. What does Andi's mother do in her free time?
   a) She works in the family business.
   b) She helps at a hospital.
   c) She is a doctor.
   d) She builds homes.

4. What does Andi's sister do?
   a) She's a homemaker.
   b) She's a nurse.
   c) She's a university student.
   d) She's a high school student.

5. When does Andi enjoy staying up late?
   a) In the morning
   b) Monday to Friday
   c) Saturday and Sunday
   d) Anytime

6. Which of these is NOT true?
   a) Andi lives in an apartment.
   b) Andi listens to music in her free time.
   c) Andi lives far from the university.
   d) Andi doesn't like getting up early on weekends.

A. Word check: *Complete this student's self-introduction. Use words from the vocabulary box below to help you.*

Hi everyone. My _____ is James Field. My _____ call me Jim. I'm nineteen _____ old and I'm _____ Sydney. I'm a _____ at Osaka University. My _____ is Japanese. I have a _____ job. I _____ in a restaurant.

My parents _____ in Sydney. My _____ is a police officer. He works very hard. My _____ is a high school teacher. She likes her job. I don't _____ any brothers or sisters. I'm an _____ child.

In my free time, I like _____ tennis and _____ to music. I play tennis two or three times a week at university. I practice from 6:00 p.m. to 8:00 p.m. I listen to rock music every day. I'm also into watching my _____ bands on the internet.

favorite	listening	work	major	part-time	live	have	from
friends	name	playing	father	student	mother	only	years

B. Grammar check: *Practice writing information about yourself.*

● **Where are you from?**

   I _____ from _____

● **Where do you live?**

   I _____ in _____

● **What does your mother / father do?**

   My mother / father _____ a _____

● **What music do you like?**

   I _____

C. Writing skill: *Writing main ideas with supporting details.*

Writing main ideas with supporting details is about expressing your thoughts in a <u>clear way</u>.
A main idea is the focus of your writing.
For example: *I like soccer.*

Supporting details then provide extra information **about the topic**.
For example: *I play soccer every week. My favorite team is ...*   ✔
                    My favorite food is pizza.   ✗

★ *Now, add extra information to your sentences in part B.*

Let's practice!

Write a main idea followed by supporting details about:

- **You: Write your name, where you are from, what you do, and where you live.**

  My name is _____ . I'm from _____ .

  I'm a _____ _____ . I live in _____ .

- **Your family: Where does your family live? What do your parents do? Do you have any brothers or sisters?**

  My family _____ in _____ .

  My _____ _____ is a _____ .

  I have / don't have any _____ .

- **Your free time: Give examples!**

  In my free time, I like _____ and _____ .

  I _____ .

Task: *Write a reply to Andi's message from page 15. Write about the following 3 things:*

Part 1: Introduce yourself (your hometown, what you do and where you live).

Part 2: Write about your family.

Part 3: Write about your free time.

Make sure each part has a main idea followed by supporting details.

★ *Use the space below to plan your writing.*

✉ Send   ⫻ Attach   🗀 Save   ✗ Cancel   ✉ 🖨
To:
Cc:
Subject:

A. Question: *What do you know about your classmates?*

For example: *With your teacher, answer the question below and fill in the boxes.*

Ex. How many females and males are in this class?

Females (Number)	Males (Number)	Females (%)	Males (%)

B. *Write the correct questions. Then ask 10 classmates and mark their answers in the tables below.*

1. How many classmates are NOT from the east of Japan?

Question: <u>Are you from the east of Japan? or Where are you from?</u>

From the east of Japan (Number)	Not from the east of Japan (Number)	From the east of Japan (%)	Not from the east of Japan (%)

2. How many classmates have B blood type?

Question: _____

Have B blood type (Number)	Don't have B blood type (Number)	Have B blood type (%)	Don't have B blood type (%)

3. How many classmates have a pet?

Question: _____

Have a pet (Number)	Don't have a pet (Number)	Have a pet (%)	Don't have a pet (%)

4. How many classmates play a musical instrument?

Question: _____

Play a musical instrument (Number)	Don't play a musical instrument (Number)	Play a musical instrument (%)	Don't play a musical instrument (%)

5. How many classmates live near the university?

Question: _____

Live near the university (Number)	Don't live near the university (Number)	Live near the university (%)	Don't live near the university (%)

C. **Results: Pie Charts** – *Pie charts are used to show your data in a clear way.*

Ex. How many females and males are in this class?

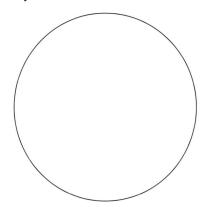

3. How many classmates have a pet?

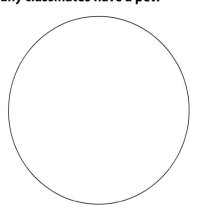

1. How many classmates are NOT from the east of Japan?

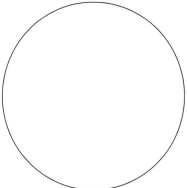

4. How many classmates play a musical instrument?

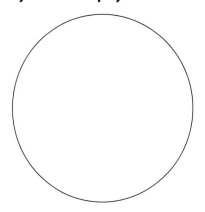

2. How many classmates have B blood type?

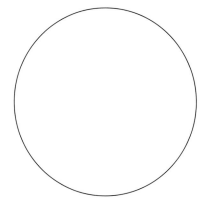

5. How many classmates live near the university?

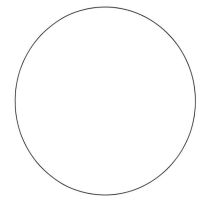

D. **Report:** *Write the results of your survey.*

For example: *Eight students in my group are from the east of Japan. Only four students have a pet.*

_____

_____

_____

_____

_____

_____

E. **Presentation:** *In groups, explain the results of your survey to your classmates using the pie charts above.*

CROSSWORD

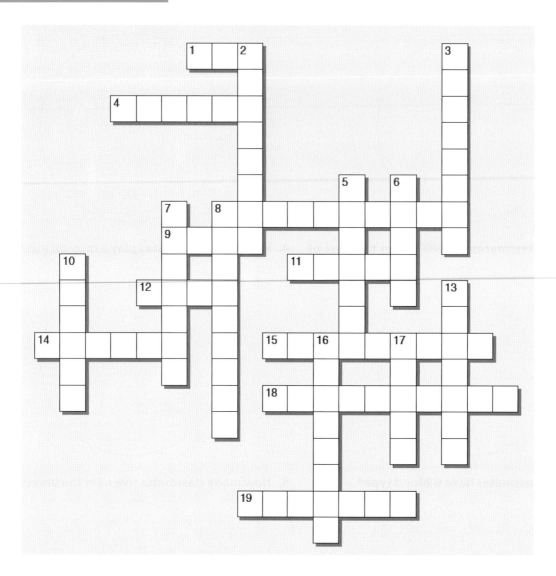

Across

1. Do you have a part-time _____?

4.

8.

9. I'm an _____ child.

11. Do you like playing _____ games?

12. I'm really _____ surfing at the moment.

14.

15. I really like _____ to music. I love J-pop.

18.

19. I don't like getting up early. I'm not a _____ person.

Down

2.   **3.**   **5.**

6. My _____ is Business.

7. What _____ are you from? France.

8.   **10.** I want to study _____ in Canada.

13. On weekends, I enjoy _____ out with friends.

16.    **17.**

MODULE 2

FOOD

Can you scan for information about food from different countries?

Can you talk about your eating habits?

Can you understand food vocabulary?

Can you use adverbs of frequency to discuss eating habits?

Can you understand a conversation about eating habits?

Can you ask and answer questions about food and drink?

Can you understand restaurant menus and restaurant reviews?

Can you write a restaurant review?

Can you find out the eating habits of your classmates?

MATCH

1. ☐

_____

2. ☐

_____

3. ☐

_____

4. ☐

_____

5. ☐

_____

6. ☐

_____

★ *Match the country with the food dishes below. Write the letter of the dish in the space next to the picture above.*

A

B

C

_____

D

E

F

_____

SCAN: Match the food with the country

A. **Scanning for information:** *In **4 minutes**, quickly read the information below to find name of each country, then write it under the shape of the country on page 22.*

B. *Read the information again and write the name of each dish under the correct food picture.* 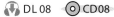 DL 08 CD08

1.

This stew of black beans, sausages and pork is called feijoada. I like to eat it with rice. I hardly ever cook it at home because it takes a long time to make. I often go out to a restaurant to eat it. People eat this dish everywhere in Brazil, but they usually eat it on Wednesdays and Saturdays, rarely on any other days.

2.

Pavlova is my favorite dessert. It is very popular in Australia. It is made from meringue with fruit and fresh cream on top. We bake it in the oven, so the outside is crunchy. I usually have it in the summer, especially at Christmas. Christmas in Australia is in the summer, so the weather is always hot!

3.

These pancakes are called hoppers in Sri Lanka. They are shaped like bowls. I always eat them for breakfast. They have an egg at the bottom, and I usually fill them with spicy curry and vegetables. I love sweet hoppers, too. They are served with honey or coconut syrup. Delicious!

4.

This is a photo of a dish called pelmeni that my mother often cooks at home. These boiled Russian dumplings are filled with minced beef or pork, or a mixture of both. The dumplings in the picture are beef because I never eat pork. I'm allergic to it. It is usually served with smetana which is similar to sour cream.

5.

This is a very simple dish of fried potatoes, cheese and gravy. Poutine is really popular in Canada, particularly in the French-Canadian province of Quebec. It is a kind of fast food, and people often eat it as a snack when they are hungry in the evening. It is fast food, but you shouldn't eat it with your hands. It's very messy!

6.

Tangyuan is a dessert that we usually eat at the Dongzhi midwinter festival (around December 22) and on the last day of the Chinese New Year (the Lantern Festival). This dish is made with colorful, sticky rice balls. It is served in a bowl with sweet ginger syrup. I always eat it at home with my family.

C. **What's your favorite dish?** *Write the name, what kind of dish it is and why you like it.*

SPEAK: Reporting and describing eating habits

A. Food expressions: *Match the expressions with the pictures below.*

_____	boiled food	_____	fast food
_____	deep fried food	_____	sweet desserts
_____	healthy food	_____	spicy food
_____	sour fruit	_____	fresh fish

B. Frequency expressions: *Write a number from 1-7 in the boxes below showing the level of frequency.*

I usually eat… ☐	I often eat… ☐	1 = 100%
I rarely eat… ☐	I never eat… ☐	
I sometimes eat… ☐	I always eat… ☐	
I hardly ever eat… ☐		7 = 0%

C. Let's talk! *In pairs, discuss your eating habits using the expressions from part B and part A.* **Try to give reasons.**

For example: **A:** *What food do you **often** eat?*

B: *I **often** eat fast food.*

A: *Me too. I **always** eat fast food because I have no money!*

VOCABULARY

DL 09 CD09

Adjectives		spicy B1	......	dinner A1	......
bitter B1	......	sweet A1	......	dish A1	......
boiled A2	......	tasty B1	......	fast food A2	......
busy A1	......	thirsty A2	......	fish A1	......
careful A1	......	unhealthy A2	......	fruit A1	......
cheap A2	......	**Adverbs (Frequency)**		lunch A1	......
closed A1	......	always A1	......	meal A1	......
delicious A1	......	hardly A2 ever A2	......	meat A1	......
expensive A1	......	never A1	......	reservation B1	......
fresh A2	......	often A1	......	service B1	......
fried A2	......	rarely B1	......	vegetable A1	......
healthy A1	......	sometimes B1	......	**Verbs**	
hungry A1	......	usually A1	......	boil A2	......
open A1	......	**Nouns**		cook A1	......
popular A2	......	breakfast A1	......	fry B1	......
salty B2	......	dessert A2	......	prefer A2	......
sour B1	......	diet A2	......	taste B1	......

A. *Match each definition with the words on the right.*

1. A meal you eat in the evening: _____
2. Plants that you can eat: _____
3. When you want something to drink: _____
4. To have a flavor: _____

a) vegetables
b) dinner
c) taste
d) thirsty

B. *Write a word with the opposite meaning to the words below.*

1. sweet _____
2. expensive _____
3. never _____
4. healthy _____

C. Give your opinion!

1. Fast food is unhealthy.
   Agree: _____ Disagree: _____
   Why? _____
2. I often eat fresh vegetables.
   Agree: _____ Disagree: _____
   Why? _____
3. I sometimes cook salty food.
   Agree: _____ Disagree: _____
   Why? _____
4. Which do you prefer, boiled food or fried food?
   _____
   Why? _____
5. What kind of diet do you recommend?
   _____
   Why? _____
6. What Japanese food do you rarely eat?
   _____
   Why? _____

GRAMMAR

Yes/No questions in the present simple with adverbs of frequency

Adverbs of frequency		Yes/No questions	
100% 0%	o always o usually o often o sometimes o rarely o hardly ever o never	Do you usually drink coffee in the morning?	No, I don't. I hardly ever drink coffee.
		Do you cook dinner at home?	Yes, I do. I usually cook Chinese food.
		Does your brother eat out with friends?	Yes, he does. He always goes out for ramen noodles.
		Does your mother eat fast food?	No, she doesn't. She never eats unhealthy food.
		Do your friends usually eat chocolate at lunchtime?	Yes, they do. They often buy chocolate at the convenience store.

A. *Fill in the blanks and then match the questions with the answers.*

1. Do _____ usually eat natto in the morning? ____
2. _____ you hungry now? ____
3. Does _____ friend often eat fast food? ____
4. _____ you healthy? ____
5. What do _____ usually eat on weekends? ____
6. What time _____ your family usually have breakfast? ____
7. What kind of food _____ you rarely eat? ____

a) We _____ have breakfast at 7:00 am.
b) I _____ eat sushi. I love fresh fish.
c) I _____ eat curry. I don't like spicy food.
d) Yes, I _____. Natto is very healthy.
e) Yes, I _____. Let's go for lunch.
f) Yes, she _____. She never cooks!
g) Yes, I _____. I eat a balanced diet.

★ *Now ask your partner the questions from part A.*

B. *Complete the sentences about you, using adverbs of frequency from the box.*

always	usually	often	sometimes	rarely	hardly ever	never

1. I _____ drink coffee in the morning.
2. I _____ drink fresh fruit juice.
3. I _____ go out to eat on weekends.
4. I _____ eat fast food.
5. I _____ cook in the evening.
6. I _____ eat spicy food.

Expressing likes and dislikes: *Providing reasons*

Providing reasons using "because ..."
I like convenience stores **because their sandwiches taste good**.
I don't like black coffee **because it's too bitter**.
I never eat fried potatoes **because they are salty**.
My mother often eats salad **because it is healthy**.

C. *Match the expressions on the left with the reasons on the right.*

1. I don't like curry because ____
2. I never eat grapefruit because ____
3. When I'm thirsty I usually drink water because ____
4. Tokyo is great because ____
5. I love living near the sea because ____
6. I like fast food because ____

a) the fish is so fresh.
b) there are so many good restaurants.
c) sweet soda drinks are unhealthy.
d) I don't like sour fruit.
e) it's cheap.
f) it tastes too spicy for me.

LISTEN

A. Pre-listening

1. *Quickly read the conversation between two students cooking dinner. Guess the missing words.*

2. *Listen to the conversation, check your answers and fill in the blanks.* 🎧 DL 10 ⊙ CD10

Jane

> Thanks for _____ dinner this evening.

> No problem. I'm making curry. It's really _____ in my country.

Anika

> Great! I sometimes eat curry at a restaurant. What's in it?

> Lots of vegetables! It's hot and _____ and is really tasty. I like cooking and eating healthy food.

> I don't have time to cook. I _____ eat instant noodles from the convenience store. I don't have much money, and I'm busy with my _____ job. Ramen is _____ but it tastes good!

B. Discussion: *What do you think about this conversation?*

> For example: "I like cooking and eating healthy food." *I understand Anika's opinion because …*
>
> "I don't have time to cook." *I understand how Jane feels because …*

C. *Listen to the rest of the conversation. Choose the correct answer from a, b or c.* 🎧 DL 11 ⊙ CD11

1. When does Anika eat curry?

  a) Monday

  b) Lunchtime

  c) Evenings

2. What does Jane eat for breakfast?

  a) Pizza

  b) Fruit

  c) Bread

3. When does Jane NOT work?

  a) Tuesdays and Saturdays

  b) Saturdays and Sundays

  c) Sundays and Mondays

D. *Listen to Jane and Anika's conversation the following week. Choose an answer a, b or c.* 🎧 DL 12 ⊙ CD12

1. When does Jane have time off work?

  a) Tuesday

  b) Tuesday and Friday

  c) Friday

2. What type of pizza will Jane make?

  a) Cheese and ham

  b) Tomato, cheese and pineapple

  c) Cheese, tomato and chicken

3. Which student probably has less free time?

  a) Anika

  b) Jane

  c) Neither is busy

E. Post-listening: *With a partner, decide what you would cook if friends came to your house for dinner.*

COMMUNICATE: What do students think?

A. *Write your answers to the questions in the "Your answer" column. Then, ask a classmate and write their answers in the "Partner's answer" column. Finally, in groups, discuss what you think is the most popular answer for university students. Write the answer in the "Most popular answer" column.*

Question	Your answer	Partner's answer	Most popular answer (Group's guess)
1. What dessert do you often eat?			
2. What vegetable do you hardly ever eat?			
3. What do you like to drink when you are thirsty?			
4. What do people often eat in the summer?			
5. What food do you think tastes sour?			
6. Name a dish that is spicy.			
7. What food is Osaka famous for?			
8. What dish are you good at cooking?			
9. What do you usually have for breakfast?			
10. Name a dish that you think is healthy.			

B. *Think of two more questions that you would like to ask about food and write them in the table below. Write your answers and then ask your classmate and complete the table.*

Question	Your answer	Partner's answer
11.		
12.		

UNIT 4 READ

A. Brainstorm

What is the name of your favorite restaurant?

Think of reasons why you like it.

My favorite restaurant is called ...

I like it because ...

B. Pre-reading: *Read the menu and try to guess the missing words.*

GREAT FOOD, GREAT SERVICE, GREAT TIMES
(10% discount for students)

FRANCO'S ITALIAN RESTAURANT

Open for breakfast, l_____ & dinner

Last orders 10:00 p.m.   Closed on Wednesdays

■ L_____ MENU ■

Starters   All $5

HOT

Minestrone soup - v_____ soup

Calamari - deep-f_____ squid

COLD

Caesar salad - lettuce, olive oil, soft-boiled egg, black olives, Parmesan cheese

Caprese salad - fresh mozzarella cheese, tomatoes, sweet basil, olive oil

Side Items   All $3

F_____ potatoes

Freshly b_____ Italian bread

Garlic rice

Boiled v_____

Drinks   All $3

COLD - f_____ orange juice, cola, lemonade, mineral water

HOT - coffee or tea

Main Courses   All $10

FRANCO'S FAMOUS PIZZA

Margherita - mozzarella cheese, tomatoes

Seafood - clams, squid, shrimp, crab

Pepperoni - s_____ Italian sausage

FRANCO'S F_____ PASTA

Carbonara - egg, bacon, Parmesan cheese

Peperoncino - s_____ chili and garlic in olive oil

Lasagna - b_____ pasta with minced beef in tomato s_____

D   All $3

Tiramisu - coffee-flavored Italian d_____

Italian chocolate cake

Panna cotta - cream pudding with raspberry s_____

Assorted Italian ice cream

C. *Check the hints in the box below and complete the menu. Then decide what you would like to eat and drink for under $20.*

| baked (x2) | dessert(s) (x2) | fresh (x2) | fried (x2) |
| lunch (x2) | sauce (x2) | spicy (x2) | vegetable(s) (x2) |

D. *Read a customer's review of Franco's restaurant. Answer the questions below.* 🎧 DL 13 ◉ CD13

PAUL'S FOOD BLOG

Hello everyone. Today I'm reviewing my favorite Italian restaurant: Franco's. I'm a regular customer at Franco's, and I often go there with my wife and kids. It is a fantastic restaurant because the meals are great! The waiters are really friendly and helpful, and the owner, Franco, always makes you feel very welcome.

The food here is the best! I love their healthy salads. I especially like the Caesar salad. The soft-boiled egg is delicious. Their deep-fried calamari tastes really good too. And the vegetables in the minestrone soup are fresh and tasty. My favorite main course is the beef lasagna. The tomato sauce is great but be careful, it's freshly baked in the oven, so it is really hot. For people who are into spicy dishes, I recommend the peperoncino pasta. If I'm still hungry, I usually have the panna cotta for dessert. The raspberry sauce is amazing. My kids always have the Italian ice cream. They love it.

Franco's is a popular restaurant, but it's not so expensive, especially the lunch menu. There is a 10% discount for students, so it's quite cheap. It's really busy on Saturdays and Sundays but not so much during the week. It's a good idea to make a reservation on weekends. They are closed on Wednesdays.

I'm definitely going to Franco's again soon! It's my birthday in three weeks and Franco's is the place I want to enjoy it.

Paul's Rating ☆☆☆☆☆

1. What do you know about Paul?
   a) He is a waiter at Franco's.
   b) He often goes to Franco's.
   c) He is the owner of Franco's.
   d) None of the above.

2. In paragraph 2, line 1, what does the word "especially" mean?
   a) Not
   b) Maybe
   c) Opposite
   d) Particularly

3. When might people need a reservation?
   a) On Wednesdays
   b) On Tuesdays
   c) During the week
   d) On Saturdays and Sundays

4. Why is this restaurant popular with students?
   a) Because it's busy.
   b) Because the prices are not expensive.
   c) Because the birthday parties are good.
   d) Because the dessert is amazing.

5. What does Paul say about the main courses?
   a) The pasta dishes are too hot and spicy.
   b) His kids love the tomato sauce.
   c) You must be careful if you are hungry.
   d) He loves the freshly baked lasagna.

6. Which of these is NOT true?
   a) It's Franco's birthday soon.
   b) It's Paul's birthday soon.
   c) Franco's is a popular restaurant.
   d) The service is good.

WRITE

A. Word check: *Complete this review of a restaurant. Use words from the vocabulary box below to help you.*

My favorite place to eat out is called "Happy Chef." It's a Western-style restaurant near my university. It's a fantastic restaurant because the food is amazing and the _____ is great.

The food is awesome! I often eat their Hamburg steak. It comes with rice or _____ potatoes. The set _____ is served with a _____ side salad. I also like the desserts at Happy Chef. I usually eat apple pie. The fruit tastes nice and _____ and the _____ cream is delicious.

I usually go to this restaurant on weekdays and it's open until 10 o'clock in the evening. It is _____ on weekends because lots of families go there. I especially like the lunch menu because it is quite _____. For 1,000 yen you can have three _____. You get a starter, a main course and a dessert. Lunch is from 11:00 a.m. to 2:30 p.m. The restaurant is _____ every Tuesday.

fried	busy	menu	sweet	healthy	service
	closed	cheap	courses	fresh	

B. Grammar check: *Practice writing about a restaurant using frequency words.*

Write about a restaurant you like.

(always / usually / often / sometimes / rarely / hardly ever / never)

- **What do you eat?**

  I _____ eat _____

- **What do you eat for dessert?**

  I _____ eat _____ for dessert.

- **When do you go there?**

  I _____ go there _____

- **Who do you go with?**

  I _____ go _____

Descriptive paragraph writing is about describing a topic and giving information about it.

First, write a main idea about the topic (topic sentence). Then, write details about it (supporting details). Try to use adjectives.

For example:

> (Topic sentence) *The food is great.* (Supporting details) *The fried potates are really tasty.*

Let's practice!

● **What's the name of your favorite restaurant? Why do you like it?**

My favorite restaurant is _____

I like it because _____

● **How is the food? Give examples.**

Their food is _____. I love their _____

I also like _____

● **When do you go there? Is it busy? Is it expensive?**

I usually go there on _____. During the week, it's _____

_____. On weekends it's _____

The prices are _____

Task: *Write a review of your favorite restaurant. Structure your writing into 3 short paragraphs.*

For example:

Paragraph 1: Describe the restaurant and give 1 or 2 reasons why you like it.

Paragraph 2: Write about the food and your favorite meals/drinks.

Paragraph 3: When do you go there? Is it busy? Is it expensive?

★ *Use the space below to plan your writing.*

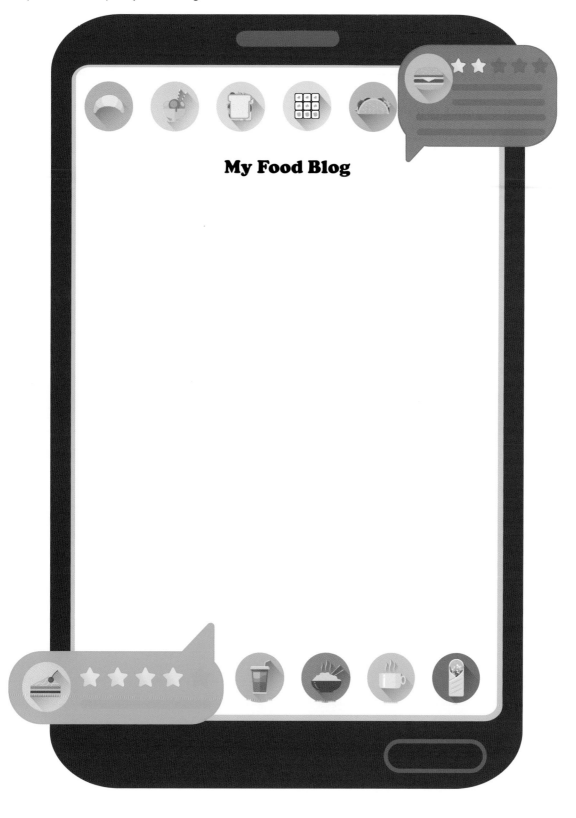

My Food Blog

PROJECT

A. Question: *What are the eating habits of your classmates?*
You are going to survey 10 classmates to find out their eating habits.

Ask 10 classmates the questions below and note their answers in the tables.

1. What do you usually eat for breakfast?

	Rice	Bread	Miso soup	Fruit	Other
No.					
%					

2. What do you usually drink in the morning?

	Coffee	Tea	Orange juice	Soda	Other
No.					
%					

3. What is your favorite dessert?

	Ice cream	Chocolate cake	Cheesecake	Strawberry shortcake	Other
No.					
%					

4. What international food do you often eat?

	Chinese	Italian	American	Indian	Other
No.					
%					

5. What restaurant do you often go to?*

					Other
No.					
%					

6. What is your favorite convenience store?*

					Other
No.					
%					

*Write the names of the most popular answers in the blue boxes.

B. Results: Column Charts - *Column charts are used to compare two or more different items.*

1. What do you usually eat for breakfast?

	Rice	Bread	Miso soup	Fruit	Other
10					
9					
8					
7					
6					
5					
4					
3					
2					
1					

4. What international food do you often eat?

	Chinese	Italian	American	Indian	Other
10					
9					
8					
7					
6					
5					
4					
3					
2					
1					

2. What do you usually drink in the morning?

	Coffee	Tea	Orange juice	Soda	Other
10					
9					
8					
7					
6					
5					
4					
3					
2					
1					

5. What restaurant do you often go to?

					Other
10					
9					
8					
7					
6					
5					
4					
3					
2					
1					

3. What is your favorite dessert?

	Ice cream	Chocolate cake	Cheesecake	Strawberry shortcake	Other
10					
9					
8					
7					
6					
5					
4					
3					
2					
1					

6. What is your favorite convenience store?

					Other
10					
9					
8					
7					
6					
5					
4					
3					
2					
1					

C. Report: *Write the results of your surveys and suggest reasons.*

For example: *In my group, 80% of students said they drink tea in the morning. I think tea is popular because it's healthy.*

_____

_____

_____

_____

D. Presentation: *In groups, explain the results of your survey to your classmates using the column charts above.*

CROSSWORD

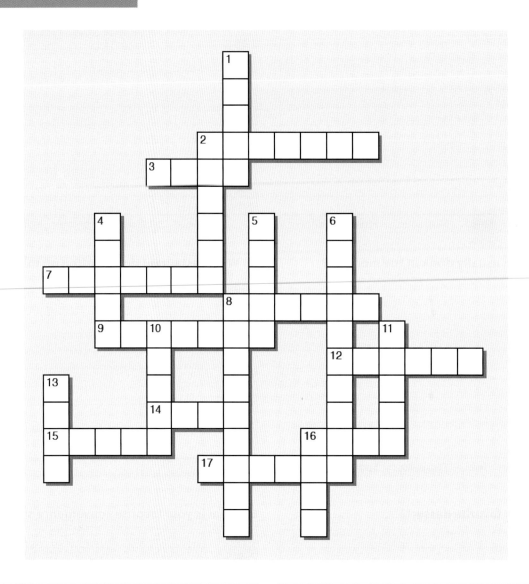

Across

2. My diet is quite _____. I rarely eat fast food.

3. I don't like grapefruit. It is really _____.

7.

8. I like milk chocolate, but I think dark chocolate is too _____.

9.

12. I _____ have coffee at breakfast. I drink it every morning.

14. I can't _____ at all. I can't even boil an egg!

15.

16.

17. The food at that new restaurant _____ really bad. Don't go there.

Down

1. I _____ eat peanuts. I'm allergic to them.

2.

4. In Japan, _____ chicken is popular at Christmas.

5.

6.

8. I don't eat _____. I'm so busy in the morning.

10.

11. _____ soda drinks are high calorie and bad for your teeth.

13.

16.

MODULE 3

FASHION

Can you scan for information about fashion styles?

Can you talk about your fashion interests?

Can you understand fashion vocabulary?

Can you express likes and dislikes when discussing fashion?

Can you understand conversations about fashion?

Can you find out about your classmates' fashion styles?

Can you read and understand people's opinions about fashion?

Can you write your opinion about the clothes you like?

Can you find out your classmates' opinions about fashion?

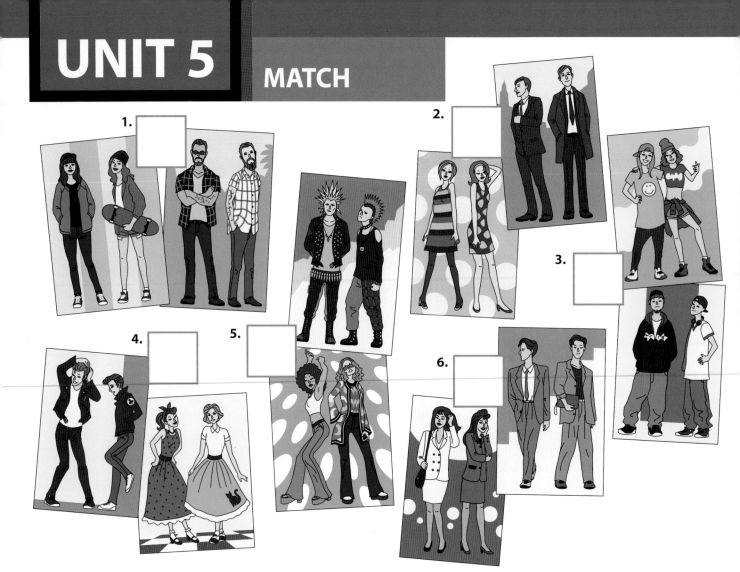

★ *Match the fashion picture with each decade below. Write the letter of the decade in the space next to the pictures above.*

_____

_____

_____

_____

_____

_____

SCAN: Match the fashion designs with the decades

A. Scanning for information: *In **4 minutes**, quickly read the information below to find key words.*

B. *Write the names of fashion trends under each decade on page 38.*

 DL 14   CD14

1.

This is the 1950s. Young people love rock n' roll music, and Elvis is popular. Young men like wearing denim jeans and white T-shirts with leather jackets. This is called rocker or greaser fashion. For teen girls, ponytails, colorful skirts and short-sleeved blouses are fashionable.

2.

The Beatles are the most famous group in the world in the sixties, and their fashion is also very popular. Men are into mod fashion and are wearing dark suits with black ties and Chelsea boots. For girls, miniskirts are stylish, and short hair is popular.

3.

Disco music is cool in the early 1970s. Flared jeans and platform shoes with high heels are in fashion. By the end of the 70s, teenagers are wearing unique styles called punk fashion and listening to punk rock music. People have their hair cut in strange Mohican styles that are dyed in bright colors.

4.

Going back to the eighties, we can see lots of designer brands and loose suits for both men and women. People like wearing suits in different colors and often wear them with T-shirts. Jackets have big shoulder designs, and women wear tight skirts. This is called yuppie fashion.

5.

In the 1990s, hip-hop is the latest fashion. People wear loose, baggy jeans, extra-large T-shirts and work boots or basketball sneakers. Also, baseball caps and hooded tops are popular. Bright-colored sports clothes are fashionable for young people.

6.

It is a new millennium and hipster fashion is the new craze. A lot of men have beards and tattoos. Tight jeans and checked shirts are trendy, and both women and men wear skater-style clothes. T-shirts and knitted caps are in fashion, and used clothing is really popular.

C. What are you wearing? *Write about the clothes you are wearing. Why do you like them?*

SPEAK: Describing likes and dislikes

A. Fashion expressions: *Match the expressions with the pictures below.*

_____	tight jeans	_____	school uniforms
_____	dyed hair	_____	loose clothes
_____	tattoos	_____	beards
_____	bright colored sneakers	_____	designer bags

A **B**  **C**  **D**

E **F** **G** **H**

B. Likes and dislikes: *Mark the expressions below with positive, negative or neutral images.*

I love…	😊😊	…look(s) cool	
I'm really into…		…look(s) stylish	
I can't stand…		…look(s) bad…	
I'm not into…		…is / are O.K.	

like

dislike

C. Let's talk! *In pairs, discuss your fashion interests. Use the expressions from part B and part A. Make sure you agree or disagree <u>with reasons</u>.*

For example: **A:** *Do you like dyed hair?*

B: *Yes, I think dyed hair **looks cool**.*

A: *Really? **I'm not into** dyed hair. <u>I like natural hair</u>.*

Bonus: Practice using your own examples.

VOCABULARY

Adjectives		tight ᴬ¹		shoes ᴬ¹	
bright ᴬ¹		unique ᴮ¹		shorts ᴬ²	
casual ᴮ¹		used ᴬ²		skirt ᴬ¹	
checked +		**Nouns**		sneakers +	
comfortable ᴬ²		bag ᴬ¹		special ᴬ¹ offer ᴬ²	
dark ᴬ¹		beard ᴮ¹		stripe ᴮ¹	
designer ᴮ²		cap ᴬ¹		style ᴬ²	
different ᴬ¹		clothes ᴬ¹		suit ᴬ²	
fashionable ᴮ¹		design ᴬ¹		sweater ᴬ²	
formal ᴮ¹		discount ᴮ¹		sweatshirt ᴮ¹	
latest ᴬ²		dress ᴬ¹		T-shirt ᴬ¹	
leather ᴬ²		earring ᴬ²		uniform ᴬ²	
loose ᴬ²		(high) heels ᴮ¹		vest +	
natural ᴬ²		jacket ᴬ¹		**Verbs**	
plain ᴮ¹		jeans ᴬ¹		suit ᴬ²	
similar ᴬ²		sale ᴬ¹		wear ᴬ¹	
striped +		sandals ᴮ¹			
stylish ᴮ¹		shirt ᴬ¹			

A. *Match each definition with the words on the right.*

1. Feels nice: _____

2. Clothes worn at school: _____

3. Something you wear on your head: _____

4. Pants made from denim: _____

a) jeans

b) cap

c) uniform

d) comfortable

B. *Write a word from the vocabulary with the opposite meaning to the words below.*

1. loose _____

2. formal _____

3. oldest _____

4. similar _____

5. dark _____

C. Give your opinion!

1. High school uniforms are a good idea.

Agree: _____ Disagree: _____

Why? _____

2. Dyed hair looks more stylish than natural hair.

Agree: _____ Disagree: _____

Why? _____

3. I prefer tight jeans to loose jeans.

Agree: _____ Disagree: _____

Why? _____

4. What do you think was the best decade for fashion?

_____

Why? _____

GRAMMAR

Expressing likes and dislikes

Questions	Likes	Dislikes
What kind of clothes do you like?	I'm really into designer clothes.	I don't like leather jackets.
What fashion does your brother like?	He likes wearing loose clothes more than tight clothes.	He can't stand wearing tight clothes.

Yes/No questions	Likes	Dislikes
Do your friends like tattoos?	Yes, they do. They love tattoos!	No, they don't. They're not into tattoos.
Is your sister interested in designer brands?	Yes, she is. She loves wearing designer clothes.	No, she isn't. She's not into expensive clothes.

A. Complete the questions and answers then match them together.

1. What _____ of fashion are you into? ____
2. What clothes does your teacher _____? ____
3. Does your mother _____ earrings? ____
4. _____ your friend like beards? ____
5. _____ you into designer bags? ____

a) Yes, she _____. She loves wearing them.
b) Yes, I am. I _____ all types of bags.
c) I'm really _____ sixties fashion.
d) No, he _____. He shaves every day.
e) She usually _____ formal suits.

★ Now, ask your partner the questions in part A.

B. Complete the sentences about you using the expressions from the box below.

love	can't stand	don't really like	enjoy	am really into	am not interested in

1. I _____ going shopping for clothes.
2. I _____ wearing bright colors.
3. I _____ reading about fashion.
4. I _____ buying clothes online.
5. I _____ used clothes designs.
6. I _____ wearing formal clothes.

Present continuous: *Talking about things you are doing now*

Questions and answers	Yes/No questions and answers
What are you wearing?	Are you wearing a tie?
I'm wearing a t-shirt and jeans.	Yes, I am. I have an interview today.
What's he wearing?	Is he wearing a hat?
He's wearing a school uniform.	Yes, he is. He is wearing a baseball cap.
What are they wearing?	Are they wearing designer clothes?
They're wearing casual clothes.	Yes, they are. They're wearing designer suits.

C. Write the correct questions then write the answers.

1. the / what / wearing / teacher / is / ?   Q: _____
   A: _____

2. you / are / wearing / clothes / new/ ?   Q: _____
   A: _____

3. your / wearing / is / classmate / sneakers / ?   Q: _____
   A: _____

★ Now, ask your partner the questions in part C.

LISTEN

A. Pre-listening

1. *Quickly read the conversation between two students about shopping. Guess the missing words.*

2. *Listen to the conversation, check your answers and fill in the blanks.* 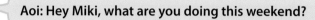 DL 16 CD16

> **Aoi: Hey Miki, what are you doing this weekend?**

> **Miki: I'm going shopping in _____! There's a sale at my favorite clothes store. I want to buy a new _____ and jeans! Aoi, do you want to come with me?**

> **Aoi: Sounds great but I'm working _____ this weekend.**

> **Miki: Me too, but I always like shopping for clothes. I love stylish new clothes. Every _____ I buy the latest _____!**

> **Aoi: Really? I like _____, but I also like to save money. I want to travel abroad next year. I also want to buy a _____, so saving money is important for me.**

B. Discussion: *What do you think about this conversation?*

| For example: "I always like shopping for clothes." | *I agree with Miki because ...* |
| "Saving money is important for me." | *I understand Aoi's opinion. I think ...* |

C. *Listen to the rest of the conversation. Choose the correct answer from a, b or c.* DL 17 CD17

1. When does the sale begin?
    a) Saturday morning
    b) Friday morning
    c) Sunday morning

2. What is the discount (%) for spending 25,000 yen?
    a) 5%
    b) 10%
    c) 20%

3. What color bag doesn't Misa want?
    a) Black and white
    b) Blue
    c) Green

D. *Listen to a conversation between Tim and a student about fashion. Choose a, b or c.* DL 18 CD18

1. Who likes tight jeans?
    a) Young people from England
    b) Tim
    c) The student

2. Who do you think prefers formal clothes?
    a) The student
    b) Tim
    c) Tim and the student both dislike formal clothes.

3. What season is the student going to England?
    a) Winter
    b) Fall
    c) Summer

E. Post-listening: *With a partner, decide what clothes you would like to buy in the next New Year sales.*

COMMUNICATE: How well do you know your classmates?

A. Look at the expressions below, then write the name of a different classmate next to each number. Then write the question in each line below.

B. Ask each student, and if you are correct, mark "o" in the box. If you are wrong, mark "x" in the box. Ask extra questions and make notes.

I guess...

1. _____ is really interested in fashion. ☐

   Q. Are you interested in fashion?

   Extra information: _____

2. _____ likes striped shirts more than plain shirts. ☐

   Q. _____

   Extra information: _____

3. _____ enjoys shopping in the January sales. ☐

   Q. _____

   Extra information: _____

4. _____ has a designer bag or wallet. ☐

   Q. _____

   Extra information: _____

5. _____ has more than 5 pairs of shoes. ☐

   Q. _____

   Extra information: _____

6. _____ is going shopping for clothes this weekend. ☐

   Q. _____

   Extra information: _____

7. _____ is wearing something new. ☐

   Q. _____

   Extra information: _____

8. _____ hates wearing formal clothes. ☐

   Q. _____

   Extra information: _____

9. _____ isn't into wearing bright colors. ☐

   Q. _____

   Extra information: _____

10. _____ prefers used clothes to new ones. ☐

    Q. _____

    Extra information: _____

UNIT 6

READ

A. Brainstorm

What clothes do you like wearing in summer / winter?

In summer, I usually wear ...

In winter, I like wearing ...

B. Pre-reading *Match the pictures with the comments below.*

Ⓐ I have a really cute designer bag.

Ⓑ I'm wearing a checked shirt.

Ⓒ I like wearing rubber sandals. I don't think they are stylish, but they are comfortable.

Ⓓ In winter, I like wearing hooded sweatshirts in bright colors.

Ⓔ I go surfing a lot, so I often wear beach shorts.

Ⓕ When I am at work, I always wear a formal business suit.

Ⓖ It is quite cold now, so I'm wearing a vest.

Ⓗ I think striped T-shirts are cool.

Ⓘ At Christmas, I always wear my favorite sweater. It's red with a funny reindeer design.

Ⓚ My favorite jacket is my leather jacket.

Ⓙ I like wearing ripped jeans because they are fashionable.

Ⓛ I love wearing my pink sneakers because they go well with my jeans.

C. *Two people are talking about fashion. Read their comments then answer the questions below.*   🎧 DL 19   💿 CD19

⭐ FASHION VOICES 🎤

(A) Mike

In summer, I usually wear casual clothes. I go surfing a lot, so I often wear beach shorts. I always wear T-shirts when it is hot. I think striped T-shirts are cool. I like them more than plain T-shirts. At the beach, I like wearing rubber sandals. I don't think they are stylish, but they are comfortable.

In winter, I like wearing hooded sweatshirts in bright colors. Today it's cold, so I'm wearing my vest. I bought it on discount. At Christmas, I always wear my favorite sweater. It's red with a funny reindeer design. I think it's really unique!

(B) Mika

At work, I always wear a formal business suit and high heels. I think formal clothes look smart. My new high heels are not comfortable, but they are stylish. Also, I have a really cute designer bag. It's expensive, but I love it.

At home, I like wearing loose clothes. Now, I'm wearing a checked shirt and ripped jeans. I like wearing ripped jeans because they're fashionable. I don't like tight jeans because they don't suit me. My favorite jacket is my leather jacket. I got it at a used clothes store. I don't wear high heels in my free time. I love wearing my pink sneakers because they go well with my jeans.

---

1. What clothes item did Mike NOT talk about?
   a) Shorts
   b) Sandals
   c) Suit
   d) Sweater

2. Why does Mike like wearing sandals?
   a) Because they are stylish.
   b) Because they are expensive.
   c) Because they feel good.
   d) Because they smell good.

3. The word "discount" in (A) is closest in meaning to:
   a) More expensive
   b) Same price
   c) Lower price
   d) None of the above

4. According to Mika, which of these is NOT true?
   a) Her new high heels are stylish.
   b) Her new high heels are formal.
   c) Her new high heels feel good.
   d) Her new high heels do not feel good.

5. The word "used" in (B) is closest in meaning to:
   a) Latest
   b) Not new
   c) New
   d) Casual

6. Why does Mika like wearing pink sneakers?
   a) Because they are formal.
   b) Because they match her suit.
   c) Because they don't match her jeans.
   d) Because they match her jeans.

WRITE

A. Word check: *Complete this student's opinion on fashion. Use words from the vocabulary box below to help you.*

I'm really _____ designer t-shirts! I think they're cool because they're so _____.
They are available in different _____. I like wearing designer t-shirts with jeans. I think
they _____ me. Today, I'm wearing a black designer t-shirt. I _____ wear this
shirt at university.

I also love wearing new sneakers. I think they're great because they feel so _____. I like
wearing sneakers with _____ designs. I always wear sneakers at university. The sneakers I'm
wearing now are white and red. I like wearing these sneakers in my _____.
Some sneakers can be expensive but there are _____ during sales.

usually	colors	discounts	different
suit	into	fashionable	comfortable	free time

B. Grammar check: *Practice expressing likes and dislikes:*

● **What do you like wearing in summer?**
I like _____
because _____

● **What do you love wearing with jeans?**
I love _____ with jeans.

● **What don't you like wearing on weekends?**
I don't _____ on weekends.

Practice writing about the clothes you are wearing now:

● **What kind of shoes are you wearing now?**
I'm wearing _____

● **What colors are you wearing now?**
I'm wearing _____

C. Writing skill: *Opinion paragraph writing*

Opinion paragraph writing is about giving your opinions on a topic. Use expressions such as "*I think...*" or "*I believe...*" Also, give reasons or supporting details to provide extra information.

For example:
I think hooded sweatshirts are cool because they look stylish, and lots of students wear them.
I like ripped jeans. I think they look good because they are fashionable.

Let's practice!

● **What clothes do you like wearing? Why do you like them? What are you wearing now?**
  (Use words from the Vocabulary page to help you).

  I think _____ are stylish. I like wearing them because they are _____

  _____. Now, I'm wearing _____.

● **What type of shoes do you like wearing? Why do you like them? What shoes are you wearing now?**
  (Use words from the Vocabulary page to help you).

  I like _____. I think they are cool because they are _____.

  Today, I'm wearing _____.

Task: *Think of clothes you like, then write about them.*
Describe the clothes and give reasons why you like them.

★ *Use the space below to plan your writing.*

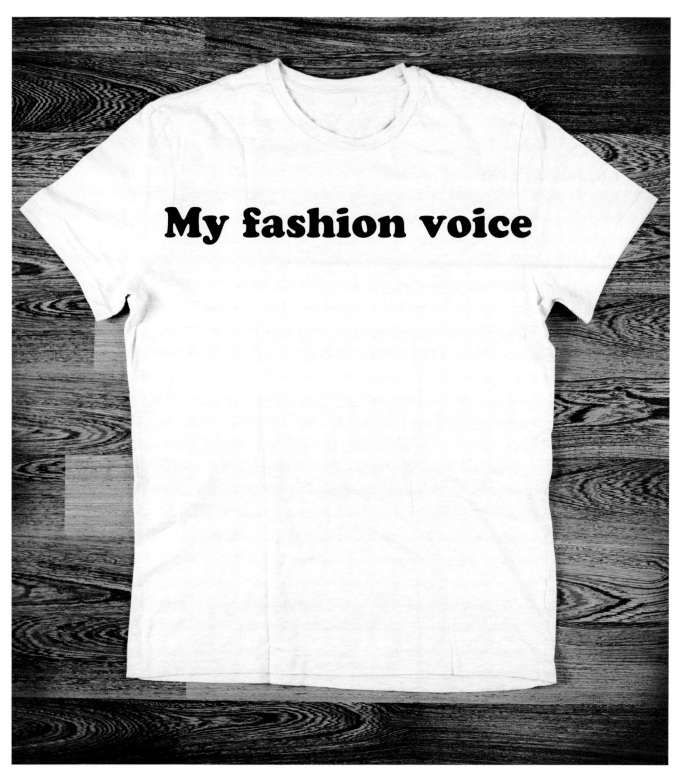

A. Question: *Do male and female students have similar fashion interests?*

Ask 10 classmates (5 males and 5 females, if possible) to give their opinion:

1. I usually wear designer clothes.

	I strongly agree (5)	I agree (4)	It depends (3)	I disagree (2)	I strongly disagree (1)	Total	Average
M							
F							

2. I can't stand wearing uniforms.

	I strongly agree (5)	I agree (4)	It depends (3)	I disagree (2)	I strongly disagree (1)	Total	Average
M							
F							

3. I rarely dye my hair.

	I strongly agree (5)	I agree (4)	It depends (3)	I disagree (2)	I strongly disagree (1)	Total	Average
M							
F							

4. I love loose clothes.

	I strongly agree (5)	I agree (4)	It depends (3)	I disagree (2)	I strongly disagree (1)	Total	Average
M							
F							

5. I'm not into tattoos.

	I strongly agree (5)	I agree (4)	It depends (3)	I disagree (2)	I strongly disagree (1)	Total	Average
M							
F							

Using Likert Scales

1. I usually wear designer clothes.

	I strongly agree (5)	I agree (4)	It depends (3)	I disagree (2)	I strongly disagree (1)	Total	Average
M			III	I	I	12	2.4
F	II	III				22	4.4

Total: Add (+) all the scores (e.g. M: 3+3+3+2+1=12; F: 5+5+4+4+4=22)

Average: Divide (÷) the total by the number of people you interviewed (e.g. M: 12÷5=2.4; F: 22÷5=4.4)

Mark each average on the chart on p. 51.

B. Results: Likert Scales & Line Charts - *Likert scales and line charts are used to show people's opinions in a clear way.*

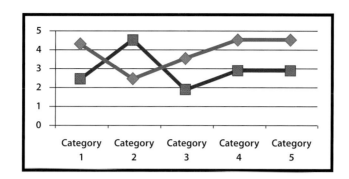

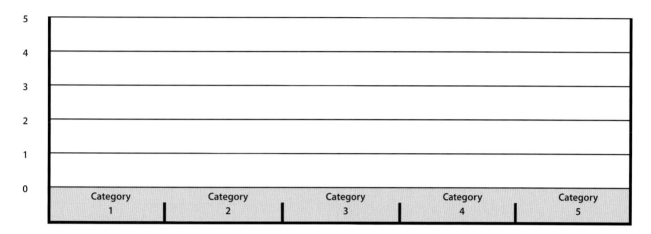

C. Report: *Write the results of your survey.*

Explain the differences and similarities of fashion opinions between males and females in your class.

For example:

- *Male students wear designer clothes more than female students.*

  For example, 4 males usually wear designer clothes, but only two females wear designer clothes.
- *Male and female students can't stand wearing uniforms.*

  For example, 5 males and 5 females can't stand wearing uniforms.
- *Male students like loose jeans more than females.*

  For example, 7 males like wearing loose jeans, but only 3 females like wearing them.

_____

_____

_____

_____

_____

_____

_____

_____

D. Presentation: *In groups, discuss your results with your classmates using the line charts above.*

CROSSWORD

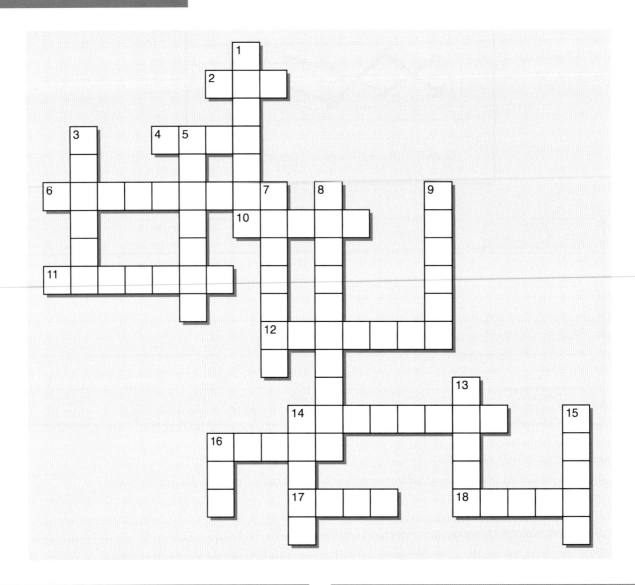

Across

2.

4. I love looking for bargains at _____ clothes stores.

6.

10. I can't _____ wearing ties.

11. I think ___ jackets look cool.

12. My jacket was cheap. It was on _____ offer.

14. I'm really into _____ brands.

16.

17.

18.

Down

1. In the summer, I often wear rubber ___.

3. Her hair is dyed blue. It looks so ___.

5.

7. My friend always wears the latest fashions. She is so ___.

8. My brother isn't ___ in fashion.

9. I like casual clothes more than ___ clothes.

13.

14.

15.

16.

MODULE 4

HEALTH

Can you scan for information about people's health?

Can you give health advice?

Can you understand health vocabulary?

Can you ask questions about health and give advice?

Can you understand conversations about health and lifestyle?

Can you talk about your health and lifestyle?

Can you read and understand people's health problems?

Can you write a letter giving health advice?

Can you find out the health differences of your classmates?

1.

2.

3.

4.

5.

★ *Look at the pictures above. Try to guess which lifestyle matches the person below. Write the letter of the person in the space in the middle of the pictures above.*

SCAN: Match the person with the lifestyle

A. Scanning for information: *In **4 minutes**, quickly read the information below to find key words, then write the name of each person's job under the correct picture on page 54.* 🎧 DL 20 💿 CD 20

1.

My name is Ken. I'm retired now, and I'm really relaxed! I really like going hiking in the mountains with my wife. I go to bed early and always get enough sleep. I eat a lot of fresh vegetables and often have salad for lunch. I love eating desserts. I eat them almost every day!

2.

I'm Nina. I love doing exercise. I go jogging almost every evening and go to the gym three times a week. I love meat, and my favorite food is steak. I eat meat every day. I also like eating fruit. I usually eat bananas after exercise. I am a high school PE teacher, so I need to keep fit.

3.

My name is Kyle. I'm not interested in sports, and I don't do any exercise. I enjoy relaxing at home and watching TV. I usually eat junk food in the evening. I'm putting on weight now. I'm a truck driver, so I spend most of the day sitting down. I'm worried about my health.

4.

I'm James, and I'm a university student. My major is Business. I work part-time as a waiter at a coffee shop. I love coffee, and I usually drink two or three cups a day. I often stay up late studying, so I don't have much free time in the morning. I never eat breakfast. I don't often go to the gym, but I go snowboarding every winter.

5.

I'm Maya. I work really hard, and I have a lot of stress. I smoke a lot, and I usually drink wine in the evening. I like playing tennis, but I can't play very often because I'm always busy at work. I'm a lawyer, so I work long hours and don't get enough sleep.

B. How healthy are you? *Write about the food you eat, how much exercise you do, and how much sleep you get.*

SPEAK: Giving health advice

A. Health expressions: *Match the expressions with the pictures below.*

_____ fruit lover		_____ stress head	
_____ exercise nut		_____ game addict	
_____ chocoholic		_____ night owl	
_____ couch potato		_____ bookworm	

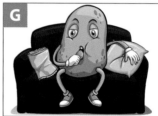

B. Giving advice: *Match the advice with the pictures above.*

Try to go to bed early for a change! ☐

Relax! Don't worry and chill out! ☐

Stop playing video games so much. You should study more. ☐

Turn off the TV and do some exercise! ☐

Watch your calories. You'll gain weight. ☐

Don't overdo it! You might hurt yourself. ☐

Great, but make sure you eat a balanced diet. ☐

Reading is good, but try to get out more. ☐

C. Let's talk! *In pairs, give advice about health. Use the expressions from part A and B.*

For example:

    A: *I'm a <u>chocoholic</u>. I love eating all kinds of chocolate, especially milk chocolate.*

    B: *Really? You should ... **watch your calories**.*

Bonus: Practice again and think of extra advice.

VOCABULARY

DL 21   CD21

Adjectives		Nouns		sore [B1] throat [B2]	
balanced [B2] (diet)	....	addict [B2]	....	stomachache [A2]	....
excited [A1]	....	cold [A1]	....	stress [B1]	....
fit [A2]	....	cough [B2]	....	vitamin [B2]	....
(high/low)-calorie +	....	dentist [A2]	....	yoga [B1]	....
lazy [A1]	....	doctor [A1]	....	**Verbs**	
negative [A2]	....	exercise [A2]	....	chill (out)+	....
positive [B1]	....	fever [A1]	....	cough [B1]	....
relaxed [A2]	....	flu [B1] (influenza)[B2]	....	exercise [A1]	....
stressed [B1]	....	hay fever +	....	feel [A1] (good/sick [A1])	....
tired [A1]	....	headache [A1]	....	gain [B1] (weight [A2])	....
Adverbs/Determiners/Pronouns		health [A1]	....	gargle +	....
enough [A2]	....	junk food [B2]	....	lose [A2] (weight [A2])	....
especially [A2]	....	lifestyle [A2]	....	quit [A2]	....
less [A2]	....	medicine [A1]	....	relax [A2]	....
more [B1 / A1]	....	protein +	....	sleep [A1]	....
once [A1]	....	rest [B1]	....	take [A1] (medicine)	....
twice [A2]	....	sleep [B1]	....	worry [A2]	....

A. *Match each definition with the words on the right.*

1. You have a fever and a headache: _____

2. A person who looks after your teeth: _____

3. The way that you live: _____

a) lifestyle

b) flu

c) dentist

B. *Fill in the blanks using words with the opposite meaning from the list above.*

- lose weight _____

- _____ high-calorie

- _____ stressed

- positive _____

C. Give your opinion!

1. Swimming is the best way to keep fit.

Agree: _____ Disagree: _____

Why? _____

2. I don't like going to the dentist.

Agree: _____ Disagree: _____

Why? _____

3. White rice is healthy.

Agree: _____ Disagree: _____

Why? _____

4. I get the flu every year.

Agree: _____ Disagree: _____

Why? _____

5. What should you do if you have a headache?

_____

_____

6. What should you do to lose weight?

_____

_____

GRAMMAR

Asking for and giving advice in the present simple using "should / shouldn't", "must / mustn't", "try to / don't"

Present tense questions and advice (Be verb)		Yes/No questions	
I have a cold. What should I do?	You should see a doctor. Don't go to class.	Should I take medicine?	Yes, you should. No, you shouldn't.
My father has the flu. What should he do?	He must go to hospital. He shouldn't go to work.	Should she take medicine?	Yes, she should.
They need to pass the test. What should they do?	They must study more. They shouldn't be absent.	Should they take medicine?	No, they shouldn't.

A. **"What should I do?"** *Match the problem with the advice.*

1. I need to gain weight. ____
2. I love eating junk food. ____
3. I'm a game addict. ____
4. I have bad hay fever. ____
5. I'm really worried about my test. ____
6. I can't get to sleep at night. ____

a) Try not to play games every day.
b) You shouldn't go out without a mask.
c) Don't stress. Chill out. Think positive!
d) You should eat more protein.
e) You mustn't use your smartphone in bed.
f) Don't eat so many burgers and try cooking at home.

★ *Now, give your own advice for each problem.*

Asking "How" questions and providing answers in the present simple

"How" questions (present tense)	Providing answers
How much fruit do you eat?	I eat a banana every day.
How much coffee does your friend drink?	She drinks two cups a day.
How many days a week do you study English?	I study English two days a week.
How many hours a week do you work?	I work 8 hours on Saturday and Sunday.
How often does your brother practice yoga?	He practices yoga three times a week.
How often do you go jogging?	I go jogging four times a week.

B. *Complete the questions, then match them with the answers.*

much   many   often

1. How _____ do you eat vegetables? ____
2. How _____ junk food do you eat? ____
3. How _____ exercise do you do? ____
4. How _____ hours do you sleep a night? ____
5. How _____ times a week do you stay up late? ____
6. How _____ do you go to the dentist? ____

a) I play tennis twice a week.
b) About 5 hours a night. I'm always tired.
c) Almost every night. I'm a night owl.
d) I eat burgers once or twice a week.
e) I have my teeth checked twice a year.
f) Every day. I love broccoli!

★ *Now, ask your partner the questions in part B.*

LISTEN

A. Pre-listening

1. *Read the conversation between two students talking about their studies. Guess the missing words.*

2. *Listen to the conversation, check your answers and complete the conversation.* DL 22 ⓞ CD22

 Hey, long time no _____! How are you?

OK. I have a test tomorrow, and there's no time to _____. I have to work later.

Yes, me too! But I'm a night _____, so when I finish my job I just stay up, have a _____ and study then.

Really? I'm not a night owl. I'm an _____ nut! I go jogging every morning, so when I finish my part-time job, I'm really _____!

Yeah, I like to stay up late, but the next day in class, I'm really _____. Maybe I should stop _____ coffee at night!

B. Discussion: *What do you think about this conversation?*

For example: "I'm not a night owl."   *I agree with her because ...*

"I like to stay up late."   *I agree with him. I think ...*

C. *Listen to the rest of the conversation. Choose the correct answer from a, b or c.* 🎧 DL 23 ⓞ CD23

1. What tests does the man have?
   a) A writing and reading test
   b) A reading and speaking test
   c) A speaking and listening test

2. Which type of test is easy for the man?
   a) Reading
   b) Listening
   c) Speaking

3. Where are the pages to study in the book?
   a) At the start
   b) In the middle
   c) At the end

D. *Listen to another conversation about health between Karen and Ken. Choose a, b or c.* 🎧 DL 24 ⓞ CD24

4. What time does Karen's job finish?
   a) 9:00 p.m.
   b) 8:00 p.m.
   c) 6:00 p.m.

5. How does Karen feel about her trip?
   a) Negative
   b) Positive
   c) Both negative and positive

6. What city does Karen probably want to see the most?
   a) New York
   b) Los Angeles
   c) Osaka

E. **Post-listening:** *With a partner, decide the best way to study for a test.*

A. First, write your answers to the questions in "Your Answer." Check your health score using the table below.

B. Next, interview 2 classmates and write their answers in the "Partner 1" and "Partner 2" columns. Check your partners' health scores.

	Your answer	Partner 1	Partner 2
1. How many nights a week don't you get enough sleep?			
A: every night B: 4 or 5 nights C: 2 or 3 nights D: I usually get enough sleep			
2. How often do you exercise?			
A: hardly ever B: a few times a month C: once or twice a week D: almost every day			
3. How many times a year do you get a cold?			
A: I never get colds B: once C: 2 or 3 times D: 4 times or more			
4. How much junk food do you eat?			
A: hardly any B: not so much C: quite a lot D: a lot			
5. How much time do you spend online or playing video games?			
A: hardly any B: 1 or 2 hours a day C: 3 or 4 hours a day D: more than 5 hours a day			
6. How often do you clean your teeth?			
A: not every day B: once a day C: twice a day D: 3 times a day or more			
7. How many sugary soda drinks do you drink?			
A: hardly any B: 1 or 2 a week C: almost every day D: 1 or more a day			
8. How many portions of fruit and vegetables do you eat a day?			
A: none B: 1 or 2 C: 3 - 5 D: 6 or more			
9. How often do you skip breakfast?			
A: every day B: 2 or 3 times a week C: 3 or 4 times a month D: never			
10. How much chocolate or sweet food do you eat?			
A: a lot B: quite a lot C: not so much D: hardly any			
Total score			

Scores:

1. A: 1 B: 2 C: 3 D: 4	6. A: 1 B: 2 C: 3 D: 4
2. A: 1 B: 2 C: 3 D: 4	7. A: 4 B: 3 C: 2 D: 1
3. A: 4 B: 3 C: 2 D: 1	8. A: 1 B: 2 C: 3 D: 4
4. A: 4 B: 3 C: 2 D: 1	9. A: 1 B: 2 C: 3 D: 4
5. A: 4 B: 3 C: 2 D: 1	10. A: 1 B: 2 C: 3 D: 4

32 – 40

Congratulations! You have a very healthy lifestyle. Keep it up!

23 – 31

Don't worry! You are pretty healthy, but you should try to improve some things.

14 – 22

You are not so healthy. You need to change your lifestyle!

UNIT 8 READ

A. Brainstorm

What is the best way to stay healthy?

For example, *eating a balanced diet, getting enough sleep, not getting a cold.*

B. Pre-reading: *Look at the pictures and write the number (1-6) of the health problem next to the correct picture below.*

① I have a bad cough.   ② I've been gaining too much weight.   ③ I have a cold.

④ I have terrible headaches.   ⑤ I have a stomachache.   ⑥ I can't get enough sleep.

Problem	Advice

Problem	Advice

Problem	Advice

Problem	Advice
1	

Problem	Advice

Problem	Advice

C. Giving health advice: *Read the advice for each problem. Write a letter (A-F) next to the correct pictures.*

Ⓐ You mustn't smoke. Try to drink hot lemon. It is good for your throat and can help you stop coughing.

Ⓑ Eating too much can make you feel sick. Don't eat spicy food, and try to relax. Stress can also cause stomach problems.

Ⓒ You should eat a balanced diet. Don't eat junk food every day. Try to exercise or play sports. This will help you lose weight.

Ⓓ You shouldn't use your phone late at night. You must try to get enough rest. You mustn't drink coffee before you go to bed.

Ⓔ Try to wear a mask when you are outside. You should take medicine and eat fruit that has a lot of vitamin C. You shouldn't go to work.

Ⓕ Don't spend too much time online. Looking at computer screens too much can give you a headache.

D. *A man has written to Doctor Collins about his health problems. Read the man's message and Doctor Collins' advice, then answer the following questions.*

(A) Dear Doctor Collins,

Recently, I have been stressed out and feeling sick. I work in a bank in Tokyo from Monday to Friday. My job makes me feel stressed because I have too much work. After work, I go home and spend hours online. I stay up late, so I can't get enough sleep, and I always feel tired the next day. I don't like cooking, so I eat junk food every day. I want to exercise, but I always feel tired, and sometimes I have terrible headaches at work. I have a cold now and a sore throat. Last week I had a fever. Recently, I have been gaining too much weight. I worry about my health so what should I do?

(B)

First, don't worry and think positive! You should change your lifestyle.

Eating a lot of junk food everyday will make you look and feel unhealthy. You should only eat junk food once or twice a week but not every day.

Not exercising is bad for your health. After work, you should exercise or play sports at the weekend. Don't spend too much time online.

Staying up late makes you feel tired. You must try to get enough rest. You should try to sleep for 7 hours each day.

Finally, eating too much junk food makes you gain weight. You should have a balanced diet. Try to eat enough fruit, vegetables, fish and meat that have lots of vitamins.

Try changing your lifestyle, and contact me again in 4 weeks. Good luck.

Dr. Cameron Collins

1. What does the man do when he finishes work?
   a) Cooks vegetables
   b) Exercises a lot
   c) Uses the Internet
   d) Sleeps

2. What health problems does the man NOT have?
   a) A headache
   b) A cold
   c) A sore throat
   d) A stomachache

3. According to the doctor, how often should the man eat junk food?
   a) Everyday
   b) 5 times a week
   c) Once or twice a week
   d) 4 times a week

4. When does the doctor tell the man to play sports?
   a) Monday to Friday
   b) Saturday and Sunday
   c) Everyday
   d) None of the above

5. What advice does the doctor give about staying up late?
   a) Think positive
   b) Eat fruit
   c) Play sports
   d) Sleep more

6. "Balanced diet" in (B) is closest in meaning to:
   a) Not eating a lot of meat
   b) Eating a lot of fruit
   c) Eating some vegetables
   d) Eating meat, fish, fruit and vegetables

WRITE

A. Word check: *A firefighter has written to a doctor about his stress. The firefighter smokes cigarettes, has no personal interests and cannot sleep well. Complete the doctor's advice. Use words from the vocabulary below to help you.*

Hello, thank you for your letter. You should change your _____.

Cigarettes are bad for your health, and they can make you feel _____. For example, cigarettes can cause cancer, bad teeth and headaches. So, you shouldn't smoke. First, try to smoke _____ each week. Then, after three weeks, try to _____ smoking.

Having no interests or hobbies can also make you feel negative and stressed. Everybody should do something in their _____ to make them feel _____. You should find a hobby that you like doing. Try to play a _____ or read an interesting _____.

Not sleeping well makes you feel _____ and causes stress. _____ late or not getting enough sleep can also lead to stress. People should get six or seven hours sleep a day. You should exercise every day, and eat a _____ of vegetables, fruit and fish. Also, don't drink too much alcohol. Having a healthy lifestyle will help you sleep well.

less	staying up	tired	book	sport	good
free time	balanced diet	quit	bad	lifestyle	

B. Grammar check: *Practice giving advice using "should / shouldn't" and "try to / don't."*

- **I'm tired. I stay up late.**

  early / go / to / bed / should / you:

  _____

- **I've been eating too much junk food.**

  diet / balanced / a / eat / to / try:

  _____

- **I smoke too much.**

  should / quit / you / to / try:

  _____

C. Writing skill: *Cause, effect and solution*

Cause, effect and solution is about writing clearly about a problem, for example "bad health." First, write about the "cause" of the problem, for example "eating junk food." Then, write about the "effect," for example "gain weight." Finally, explain the "solution," for example, "have a balanced diet."

Make a list of different causes, effects and solutions for "health problems."

Cause	Effect	Solution
Eating junk food	Gain weight	Have a balanced diet

Next, write a topic sentence about the cause _and_ effect. Then write supporting details **and** give solutions using **"should / shouldn't / try to / don't."**

For example:

Eating junk food makes you *gain weight*. For example, potato chips and candy are high-calorie. Also, eating instant noodles is unhealthy. You should *have a balanced diet*. Try to eat fruit, vegetables and fish every day.

_____ makes you _____

For example, _____

You should / shouldn't _____

Task: *Giving advice.*

Brad is a hotel manager. He is stressed. He works from morning to evening every day. He has no free time. He stays up late and is always tired. After work he drinks alcohol.

Write a letter giving advice. Write a topic sentence and give supporting details for each health problem.

★ *Use the space below to plan your writing.*

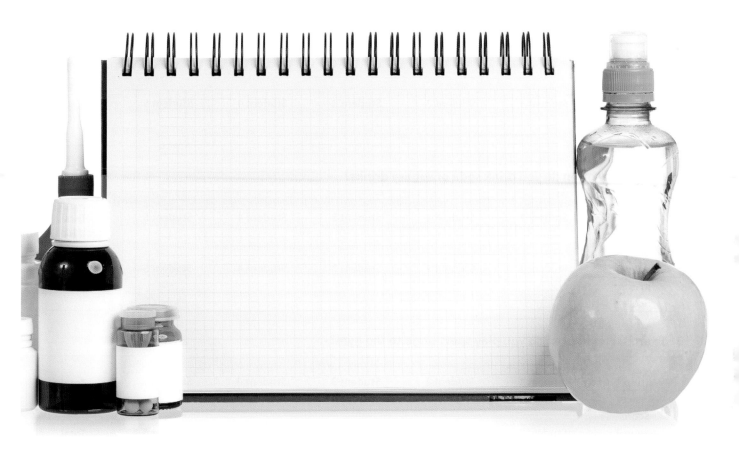

PROJECT

A. Question: *Who has the healthier lifestyle?*

Choose two different groups. For example, Group 1: Japanese students, Group 2: International students.

Ask 10 students (5 from each group) about the following health topics: food, drink, exercise, sleep and stress.

Ask the students the questions below and note their answers (A, B, C or D) and their scores (1, 2, 3 or 4) in the tables.

Write the total for each question.

1. Food: How much junk food or unhealthy food do you eat?

A: a lot, I love it! B: quite a lot C: not so much D: hardly any, I don't like it! (A=1, B=2, C=3, D=4)						
Group 1	Student 1	Student 2	Student 3	Student 4	Student 5	Total /20
Answer						
Score						
Group 2	Student 1	Student 2	Student 3	Student 4	Student 5	Total /20
Answer						
Score						

2. Drink: How often do you drink soda or sugary drinks?

A: every day B: 2 or 3 times a week C: 3 or 4 times a month D: hardly ever (A=1, B=2, C=3, D=4)						
Group 1	Student 1	Student 2	Student 3	Student 4	Student 5	Total /20
Answer						
Score						
Group 2	Student 1	Student 2	Student 3	Student 4	Student 5	Total /20
Answer						
Score						

3. Exercise: How often do you play sport or go to the gym?

A: 2 or 3 times day B: once a day C: 3 or 4 times a week D: hardly ever (A=4, B=3, C=2, D=1)						
Group 1	Student 1	Student 2	Student 3	Student 4	Student 5	Total /20
Answer						
Score						
Group 2	Student 1	Student 2	Student 3	Student 4	Student 5	Total /20
Answer						
Score						

4. Sleep: How many hours a night do you usually sleep?

A: about 8 hours B: 6-7 hours C: about 5 hours D: less than 5 hours (A=4, B=3, C=2, D=1)						
Group 1	Student 1	Student 2	Student 3	Student 4	Student 5	Total /20
Answer						
Score						
Group 2	Student 1	Student 2	Student 3	Student 4	Student 5	Total /20
Answer						
Score						

5. Stress: How much stress do you have?

A: a lot B: quite a lot C: not a lot D: no stress (A=1, B=2, C=3, D=4)						
Group 1	Student 1	Student 2	Student 3	Student 4	Student 5	Total /20
Answer						
Score						
Group 2	Student 1	Student 2	Student 3	Student 4	Student 5	Total /20
Answer						
Score						

B. Results: Radar / spider charts – *These charts are used to show a person's strengths and weaknesses.*

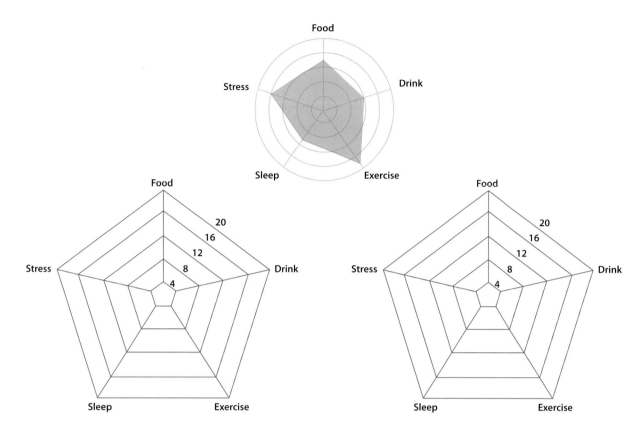

Group 1: _____

Group 2: _____

C. Report: *Write the results of your survey.*

1. Report the results from part B. Explain any differences between the health of Group 1 and Group 2.

2. Give advice on any problems from your data.

For example:

International students drink more sugary drinks than Japanese students. For example, 5 International students drink sugary drinks twice a day but only 1 Japanese student drinks sugary drinks. I think International students should drink Japanese tea because it is very healthy.

_____

_____

_____

_____

_____

_____

_____

_____

D. Presentation: *In groups, explain the results of your survey to your classmates using the radar/spider charts above. Check your results with the other groups.*

CROSSWORD

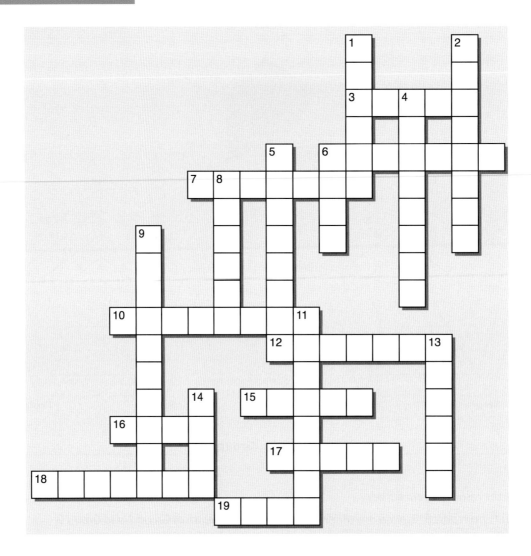

Across

3.

6.

7. You shouldn't eat so much high-____ junk food. You'll gain weight.

10.

12. I'm very ____ about my trip to New York. I love traveling.

15. Don't ____ about it. Try to relax!

16.

17.

18. I eat a lot of fresh fruit and vegetables. I like ____ food.

19. I'm trying to ____ weight. I want to be slimmer.

Down

1.

2. I get really ____ during my final exams. I'm so nervous.

4.

5.

6. Food is important for your health. You should eat a balanced ____.

8. I'm always online. I'm an internet ____.

9.

11. I often play sport and ____ at the gym.

13.

14. You should study harder. Don't be so ____!

MODULE 5

TRAVEL

Can you scan for information about famous places?

Can you talk about your past vacations or trips?

Can you understand travel vocabulary?

Can you use 'past' questions about travel and give answers?

Can you understand conversations about vacations?

Can you answer questions about travel in general?

Can you read and understand postcards and vacation reviews?

Can you write about a trip you had?

Can you find out about your classmates' favorite trips in Japan?

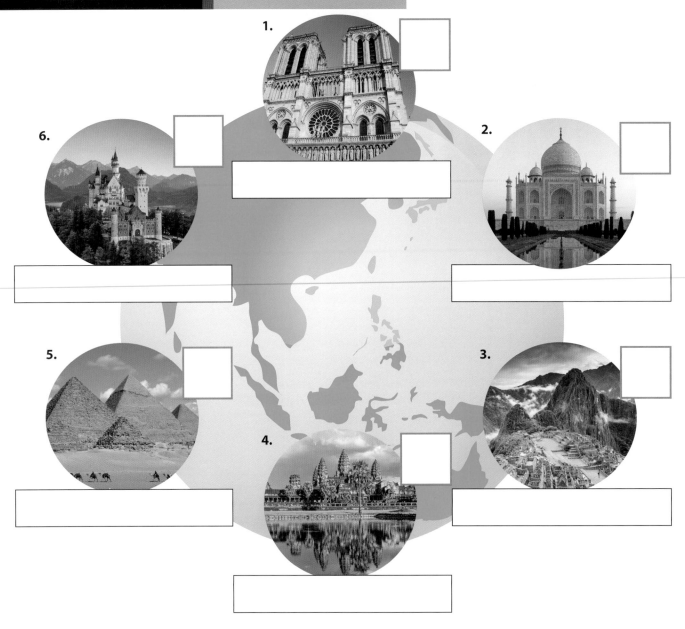

★ *Look at the pictures above. Try to guess which famous sightseeing place matches each country below. Write the letter next to the picture above.*

SCAN: Name the famous places

DL 26   CD26

A. Scanning for information: *In **4 minutes**, quickly read the information below to find key words.*

B. *Write the names of the famous places under the correct picture on page 70.*

1.

I had a great vacation in France. I did so much sightseeing in Paris. I visited lots of famous museums and ate some amazing food. I climbed to the top of the Eiffel tower. The view was amazing. I also went to Notre Dame, the famous cathedral in the center of Paris. I bought my parents some wine as a souvenir.

2.

Last year, I visited India for the first time. It is an incredible country, but the weather was so hot and humid. The food was also very hot. I love spicy curry, so I really enjoyed the food. The best place I visited was the Taj Mahal. It is a UNESCO World Heritage Site and one of the most beautiful buildings in the world.

3.

I really wanted to go to Machu Picchu, so I flew to Peru last December. It rained quite a lot, and it was cloudy at the top of the mountain. I took a train to Machu Picchu and then went trekking along the Inca Trail. The scenery was fantastic. I bought alpaca wool hats and scarves for my friends.

4.

My best vacation ever was when I went to Angkor Wat. Angkor Wat is a huge temple near the town of Siem Reap in Cambodia. I stayed in a hotel with a large pool. The staff at the hotel were great, and the people I met were so friendly. I had a really good tour guide who showed me around, and we even went to a jungle temple. Later, I went on a cycling tour of the local villages.

5.

During the spring holiday, I went on a group tour to Egypt. First, we took a sightseeing bus to Luxor, and then we returned to Cairo. From Cairo we visited the Pyramids of Giza. We rode on a camel in the desert before returning to the hotel. The weather was very hot during the day, but it was quite cool at night.

6.

I studied abroad in Germany for three months. I stayed with a homestay family in Munich. At the weekend, we often went to the park for a picnic and ate German sausages. I also went on a river cruise. The most beautiful place I visited was Neuschwanstein Castle. It looks like the Sleeping Beauty Castle. I took a lot of photographs and sent my friends postcards of the view.

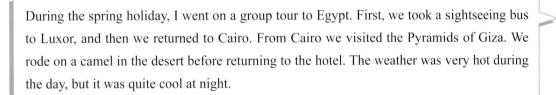

C. Your favorite trip: *Write about where you went, who you went with, where you stayed and what you did.*

SPEAK: Reporting on past vacations

A. Vacation expressions: *Match these expressions with the pictures below.*

_____	We ate lobster.	_____	I bought koala toys.
_____	The weather was nice and sunny.	_____	We stayed in a really nice hotel.
_____	The flight was long and tiring.	_____	The scenery was amazing!
_____	I went surfing.	_____	We saw the Sydney Opera House.

 A
 B
 C
 D

 E
 F
 G
 H

B. Holiday questions: *Match the questions below with the expressions above.*

_____	How was the weather?	_____	Where did you stay?
_____	What did you do?	_____	What did you eat?
_____	What souvenirs did you buy?	_____	What did you see there?
_____	How was the journey?	_____	How was the scenery?

C. Let's talk! In pairs, talk about trips you enjoyed in Japan or abroad. First, try the example below then talk about your own experiences:

A: *I enjoyed my trip to <u>Australia</u>.*

B: *Cool! How was the weather?*   **A:** *The weather was <u>nice and sunny</u>.*

B: *How was the journey?*   **A:** *The flight was <u>long and tiring</u>.*

B: *Where did you stay?*   **A:** *We stayed <u>in a really nice hotel</u>.*

B: *What did you do?*   **A:** *I went <u>surfing</u>.*

B: *What did you see there?*   **A:** *We saw <u>the Sydney Opera House</u>.*

B: *How was the scenery?*   **A:** *It was <u>amazing</u>.*

B: *What did you eat there?*   **A:** *We ate <u>lobster</u>.*

B: *What souvenirs did you buy?*   **A:** *I bought <u>koala toys</u>.*

VOCABULARY

⬇ DL 27   ◎ CD27

Adjectives

amazing B1	castle A2	sightseeing A2
exhausting B2	cathedral B2	souvenir B1
fantastic A2	check-in B1	temple A1
humid B1	countryside A2	tour A2
local A2	cruise A2	tourist A2
luxurious B2	customs B1	transportation B1
spectacular B1	departure B1	trip A1
stunning B1	destination B1	vacation A1
wonderful A1	flight A2	view A2
	guidebook A2	weather A1

Nouns

accommodation B2	holiday A1	**Verbs**
airport A1	hiking A2	arrive A1
arrival B1	homestay +	drive A2
backpacking B1	hostel B1	fly A1
baggage B1	immigration B1	stay A1
beach A1	journey A2	take A1 (a train A1)
bus A1	passport B1	travel A1
camping A2	scenery A2	visit A1
	shrine +	

A. *Match each definition with the words on the right.*

1. Visiting interesting places as a tourist: _____

2. Form of travel from place to place: _____

3. A gift bought on vacation: _____

4. The place where passports are checked: _____

a) immigration
b) souvenir
c) transportation
d) sightseeing

B. *Circle the word that does NOT belong in the list.*

- At the airport: immigration   customs   countryside   check-in
- Vacation: holiday   trip   tour   cathedral
- Accommodation: baggage   hotel   homestay   hostel

C. Give your opinion!

1. Hokkaido has the most amazing scenery in Japan.
   Agree: _____   Disagree: _____
   Why? _____

2. When abroad, you should eat the local food.
   Agree: _____   Disagree: _____
   Why? _____

3. To improve your English, you should study abroad.
   Agree: _____   Disagree: _____
   Why? _____

4. Summer is the best time to go camping.
   Agree: _____   Disagree: _____
   Why? _____

5. The shinkansen is the best form of transportation.
   Agree: _____   Disagree: _____
   Why? _____

6. What is the most spectacular castle in Japan?
   _____
   Why? _____

Asking and answering questions about trips in the past simple

Past tense questions (Be verb)		Past tense Wh- questions (Other verbs)	
		What did you do?	I went backpacking.
How was the weather?	It was cloudy.	What did you eat?	I ate spaghetti.
		Why did you like it?	The scenery was amazing.
How was the hotel?	It was really nice.	Where did you stay?	We stayed in a hostel.
		When did you arrive?	We arrived on Tuesday.
How was the food?	It was delicious!	When did you come back?	I came back on Friday.
		Who did you go with?	I went with my brother.
Yes/No questions (Be verb)		**Yes/No questions (Other verbs)**	
Was the holiday fun?	Yes, it was. I had a great time.	Did you enjoy the flight?	Yes, I did. The service was good.
Was the weather cold?	No, it wasn't. It was quite warm.	Did your wife like the food?	Yes, she did. She loved it.
Was the food tasty?	Yes, it was. I loved the fresh pasta.	Did they have a good time?	Yes, they had a great time.

A. *Write the verbs in the past tense.*

1. buy   _____

2. have   _____

3. eat   _____

4. drink   _____

5. go   _____

6. be   _____

7. take   _____

8. enjoy   _____

9. visit   _____

10. travel   _____

B. *Complete the questions below using the past tense.*

1. Where _____ your family go on vacation? ____

2. _____ your sister buy any souvenirs? ____

3. What kind of food _____ your friend eat? ____

4. _____ the weather sunny? ____

5. How _____ the scenery? ____

a) Yes, she _____. She _____ some stuffed toys.

b) It _____ beautiful. I _____ a lot of photographs.

c) No, it _____. It rained a lot.

d) They _____ to Hawaii. They _____ a great time.

e) He _____ a lot of local food. He _____ the sausages.

C. *Put the questions and answers in correct order, then match them together.*

1. Did you buy a souvenir last vacation? ____

2. Where did you go on holiday last year? ____

3. Where did you eat lunch yesterday? ____

4. Did you stay at a hotel last year? ____

5. Did you visit a shrine last month? ____

a) Kyoto / went / I / to

_____

b) yes / went / in / I / shrine / Narita / to / a

_____

c) I / didn't / go / no / shopping

_____

d) ate / the / in / I / lunch / hotel / restaurant

_____

e) didn't / I / no / . / I / hostel / stayed / in / a

_____

★ *Now, ask your partner the questions in part C.*

LISTEN

A. Pre-listening

1. *Read the conversation between two office workers talking about a trip abroad. Guess the missing words.*

2. *Listen to the conversation, check your answers and complete the conversation.* ⬇ DL 28   ◎ CD28

> So David, you're back from your trip to Sydney. How was it?

> Mizuki, I had a great time! I love _____ !

> Really? How _____ the weather?

> It was sunny but _____ . I went to the beach a lot, and I _____ surfing. In the evenings, we _____ in really nice restaurants. They were expensive though!

> Sounds great! I wish I could go to Sydney but it's so far away and I don't think my _____ is good enough.

> You should go. I _____ lots of Japanese people there and there were lots of Japanese restaurants! Next time, you should come with me!

B. Discussion: *What do you think about this conversation?*

For example:

"I wish I could go to Sydney."   *I agree with Mizuki because ...*

C. *Listen to two travel announcements. Choose the correct answer from a, b or c.*

Announcement 1   ⬇ DL 29   ◎ CD29   **Announcement 2**   ⬇ DL 30   ◎ CD30

1. Why did the man probably sleep well?

   a) The rooms were nice.

   b) The rooms were big.

   c) The rooms were quiet.

4. When should you check in for international flights?

   a) At least 45 minutes before take-off

   b) At least 1 hour and 45 minutes before take-off

   c) At least 40 minutes before take-off

2. What time does breakfast finish on weekdays?

   a) 11:00 a.m.   b) 9:00 a.m.   c) 10:00 a.m.

5. What can't you take through security?

   a) Drinks   b) Passport   c) Tobacco

3. What do you think the man enjoyed doing the most?

   a) Using the gym

   b) Using the swimming pool

   c) Walking in the hotel garden

6. Where can people smoke inside the airport?

   a) At the departure gate

   b) At customs

   c) In smoking rooms near the departure gates

D. Post-listening: *Where did you go on your last vacation or trip? Describe it to your partner.*

Did you go to an amusement park last year?	Who did you spend last New Year's holiday with?	Name the six countries at the beginning of Module 2.	**TRAVELOPOLY RULES** In groups of three or four, use a pencil, and without looking, touch one of the dice in the box. Check the number, move that number of spaces and answer the question.		

Name the five countries at the beginning of Module 1.		Catch an express train, go forward 4 spaces	Did you travel anywhere by plane last year?	When was the last time you went on vacation?	Name the six countries at the beginning of Module 5.	Did you buy any souvenirs on your last trip?

Travelopoly

Taxi gets a flat tire, go back 2 spaces				What did you do last summer vacation?
When did you last travel abroad?	Did you go skiing or snowboarding last winter?	Name three countries in Europe beginning with the letter "S."	Oh no, miss the bus to the airport. Go back 5 spaces	Did you visit a temple or shrine on New Year's Day this year?
Did you go anywhere by ship or ferry last year?	**Arrival**	What was your best ever trip or vacation in Japan?		Long wait at immigration, go back 2 spaces
Disaster! You lose your passport. Go back to Departure		Did you go to a festival last year?		Where did you go on your high school trip?
Did you go anywhere nice in Golden Week?		Name four World Heritage Sites in Japan.		Did you go to the beach last year?

Name five capital cities in Asia.	Decide to stay an extra night. Skip one turn	Did you stay in a hotel last year?	What did you eat on Christmas Day last year?	A friend takes you sightseeing. Go forward 2 spaces	**Departure**

UNIT 10 READ

A. Brainstorm

Where did you go on your last trip in Japan / abroad?

What did you do? How was the weather? What did you eat?

B. Pre-reading

Postcard from Hawaii - Partner A

In pairs, partner (A) looks at the postcard on page 77, partner (B) looks at the same postcard on page 78. Ask your partner for hints for the missing words next to each number.

For example - Partner (A): "Number 6." Partner (B): "They are gifts."

Hi, how are you doing? I'm on vacation in Hawaii. I arrived two days ago. I

1 _____flew_____ direct. The flight was good. It 2 _____ six

hours from Tokyo. On the first day, I went 3 _____shopping_____ at the Ala

Moana Center. I 4 _____ some great beach 5 _____shorts_____

and 6 _____ . After that, I 7 _____ate_____ dinner at a

live music Cafe and I 8 _____ fresh pineapple 9 _____juice_____ . The food was

10 _____ . Yesterday, the 11 _____weather_____ was very hot and sunny, so in the

morning I went 12 _____ . In the afternoon, I went 13 _____hiking_____ and

14 _____ to the top of Diamond Head. The view was 15 _____amazing_____ . Last night I

16 _____ to the hotel 17 _____restaurant_____ and 18 _____ Hawaiian food.

The Kalua pork was so good. I'm having a great time. You should come here! See you when I get back to

Japan.

Postcard from Hawaii - Partner B

In pairs, partner (A) looks at the postcard on page 77, partner (B) looks at the same postcard on page 78. Ask your partner for hints/gestures for the missing words next to each number.

For example - Partner (A): "Number 6." Partner (B): "They are gifts."

Hi, how are you doing? I'm on vacation in Hawaii. I arrived two days ago. I ₁ _____

direct. The flight was good. It ₂ _____took_____ six hours from Tokyo. On the first day, I went

₃ _____ at the Ala Moana Center. I ₄ _____bought_____ some great beach

₅ _____ and ₆ ___souvenirs___ . After that, I ₇ _____ dinner at a

live music Cafe and I ₈ _____drank_____ fresh pineapple ₉ _____ . The food was

₁₀ ____delicious____ . Yesterday, the ₁₁ _____ was very hot and sunny, so in the

morning I went ₁₂ _____swimming_____ . In the afternoon, I went ₁₃ _____ and

₁₄ ____climbed____ to the top of Diamond Head. The view was ₁₅ _____ . Last night

I ₁₆ _____went_____ to the hotel ₁₇ _____ and ₁₈ _____tried_____ Hawaiian

food. The Kalua pork was so good. I'm having a great time. You should come here! See you when I

get back to Japan.

C. *Read a tourist's review of their trip to Dubai. Answer the following questions.* ⬇ DL 31 ◉ CD31

DUBAI

Last year, I went on vacation to Dubai with my friends. We had an amazing time. We stayed in a really luxurious hotel. Our rooms were really big, and the hotel had 3 swimming pools. My room was on the top floor, and the view from my window was spectacular.

The weather in Dubai was really hot and humid, but I did a lot of sightseeing. We went to a waterpark which was so much fun. We went on lots of water rides, and I bought a souvenir t-shirt. My favorite part of the trip was taking a river cruise. We saw lots of beautiful temples and the famous Burj Khalifa, the world's tallest building, which was stunning. We didn't go to the top of the Burj, but we did take a helicopter ride, and we took some wonderful photos.

Dubai was very hot, so we didn't walk outside much in the daytime, but we walked a lot in the evenings. There were lots of interesting markets, and I bought some clothes that were great bargains. We also ate at some fantastic restaurants without needing to make reservations. There was a lot of ethnic food, and I enjoyed eating Indian food the most.

The trip was great, but the journey was exhausting. The flight was 10 hours, and the plane was delayed for 2 hours. The flight service was OK, but I didn't really like the food. When we arrived at the airport, there were really long lines at customs. There was also a lot of traffic when we left the airport, so we checked into our hotel late in the evening. Still, we loved Dubai!

1. The word "luxurious" in paragraph 1 on line 2 is closest in meaning to:

a) Small   **c)** Expensive

b) Big   **d)** Friendly

2. What did the tourist enjoy doing the most?

a) Taking a helicopter ride

b) Taking a boat cruise

c) Seeing the markets

d) Going shopping

3. The word "bargains" in paragraph 3 on line 3 is closest in meaning to:

a) Expensive

b) Old

c) New

d) Good value

4. What was the problem at customs?

a) The food was bad.

b) A lot of people were waiting.

c) People were angry.

d) Someone lost their passport.

5. When did the tourist walk around Dubai?

a) In the morning

b) In the afternoon

c) In the evening

d) Anytime

6. Which of these is NOT true?

a) The flight was long.

b) The tourist climbed the Burj.

c) The tourist enjoyed Dubai.

d) The scenery was fantastic.

A. Word check: *Complete this review of a camping trip. Use words from the vocabulary box below to help you.*

Last _____, I went camping in Miyazaki with my friends. It was _____!
We stayed at a great camp site. The _____ was beautiful. It was next to a really nice
_____, and there were lots of people surfing. Our tent was nice too. It was big and
_____.

We did a lot of exercise. There was a big mountain near the campsite. So, in the mornings we
ate breakfast and then went _____. In the afternoons we swam in the ocean and
_____ on the beach. The _____ was hot! We also went cycling. In the
evenings, we had a barbecue. The food was _____.

The journey was good. It only took about three hours by _____. My friend drove. We
started the journey at about 9:00 a.m. and arrived in time for _____. I really loved my
camping trip to Miyazaki!

lunch	beach	summer	car	delicious	weather
relaxed	hiking	comfortable	scenery	fantastic	

B. Grammar check: *Practice writing about trips in the past simple.*

Last year, I (travel) _____ to Thailand with my friends. It (be)_____ amazing!
We (stay) _____ in a really nice hotel. It (have)_____ a really big swimming pool.
The view from my room (be)_____ stunning.

We (do)_____ a lot of sightseeing. We (see) _____ many temples. We also
(go) _____ on a boat cruise. I (take)_____ a lot of photos. I (like) _____
going shopping, too. I (buy)_____ a lot of clothes! At night, we (eat) _____ in
fantastic restaurants. The local food (taste)_____ a little spicy but I (love)_____ it!

The flight (take) _____ about 5 hours, but I (enjoy) _____ it. The service (be)
_____ good. I (watch) _____ two movies and (drink)_____ tea. I also
(sleep) _____ a little.

C. Writing skill: *Mind-mapping*

Mind-mapping can help you plan your ideas in a clear way <u>before</u> you start writing. First, think of the main ideas that you want to write about. Then, think of supporting details and link them together. When you have finished, your mind map will show you all the information you need to write about in a clear way.

For example: *Look at the mind map below that was used to plan the writing about Dubai on page 79 . Complete the missing information by filling in the blanks.*

Draw your own mind map about a trip you had in Japan or abroad. Think of supporting details about the same topics.

Task: *Use your mind map to help you write clearly about a trip you had in Japan or abroad. Write 3 short paragraphs:*

Paragraph 1: Where did you go? How was the accommodation?

Paragraph 2: What did you do?

Paragraph 3: How was the journey?

Remember to write in the past tense.

★ *Use the space below to draw your mind map and plan your writing.*

AIR MAIL   POSTCARD

PROJECT

A. Question: *Where are popular places to take a trip in Japan?*

Ask 10 students about their best trip in Japan. Use "past" questions from the "Holiday questions" on p. 72. Find out reasons for students answers. Check your results and write about any similarities or differences in part B.

Interviews

	1. Where did you go?	2. Why did you like it?	3. What did you do?	4. What did you eat there?	5. What souvenirs did you buy?
1					
2					
3					
4					
5					
6					
7					
8					
9					
10					
Results					

B. Report: *Write about any similarities or differences in your results. Try to use main ideas and supporting details. Also, use the past tense when giving supporting details.*

For example: *University students enjoy different trips in Japan. For example, three students went to Okinawa, three students went to Kyoto, two students went to Nigata and two students went to Osaka.*

C. Presentation: *In groups, explain the results of your interviews to your classmates.*

CROSSWORD

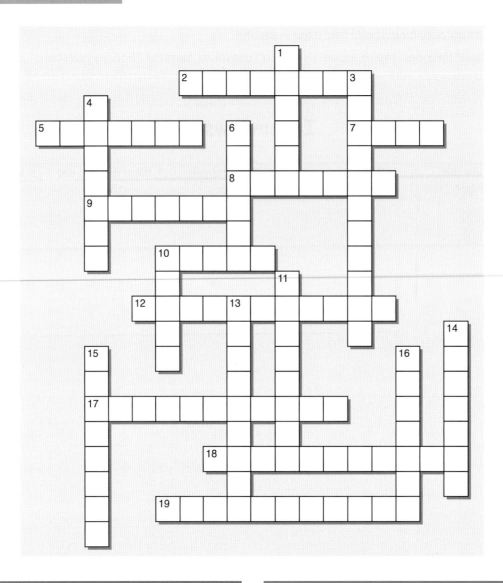

Across

2. I bought a koala toy as a ____ .

5. How was the ____ ? Terrible! It rained all day!

7. Where did you ____ ? In a nice local hostel.

8. The mountain ____ was so beautiful. I took lots of photographs.

9.

10.

12.

17.

18.

19.

Down

1. I think Kiyomizu-dera is the most famous ____ in Japan.

3. That restaurant is really popular. You need to make a ____ .

4.

6.

10. Summer is so hot and ____ in Japan.

11. Where did you go on your last ____ ?

13. I bought a great ____ . It had lots of advice on local restaurants and the best places to visit.

14. The train ____ takes about 1 hour.

15.

16.

MODULE 6

RULES

Can you scan for information about rules?

Can you talk about rules in Japan and around the world?

Can you understand rules vocabulary?

Can you use modal verbs to discuss rules?

Can you understand conversations about rules?

Can you talk about rules and customs around the world?

Can you read and understand high school and university rules?

Can you write about the rules at your high school and university?

Can you find out important university rules from your classmates?

1.

6.

2.

7.

5.

4.

3.

★ *Look at the signs above. Try to guess which sign matches each picture below. Write the letter next to the sign above.*

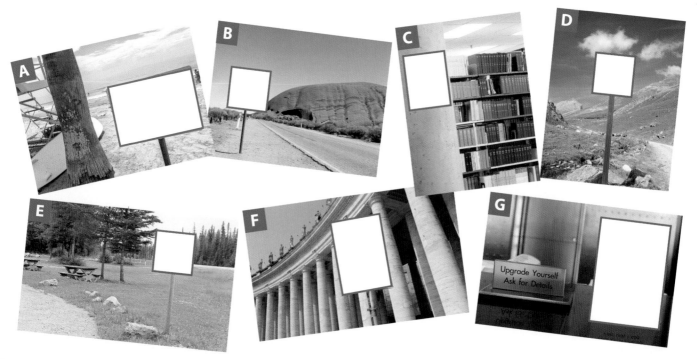

SCAN: Where would you see these signs?

A. Scanning for information: *In **4 minutes**, quickly read the information below to find key words.*

B. *Write the place you would see these signs under the correct picture on page 86.* 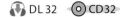 DL 32   CD32

1.
A brown sign represents leisure information. This sign means that people can have picnics here. There are usually special picnic areas in parks. But, remember, you must take your garbage home with you.

2.

If you see this sign, you must slow down and drive carefully. It means there are wild animals in this area. There are many different animal warning signs all around the world, but you only see this kangaroo sign in Australia.

3.
You are not allowed to camp where you see this sign. This sign means that this place is not a campsite, so you mustn't put up tents here. You often see these signs on private land, national parks and mountain areas.

4.

In South-east Asian countries, you can see these signs in hotels, airports, shopping centers and on public transportation, such as buses. You mustn't take durian fruit into any place where you see this sign because durians have a very strong smell.

5.
A red circle with a red line across it is used to warn people of something they are not allowed to do. This sign means that people mustn't talk loudly. You usually see this sign in libraries and other places where you should speak quietly.

6.

You can walk dogs on the beach, but in places where you see this sign, you must keep your dog on a leash. You mustn't let your dog run around freely, because it might disturb other people. Also, please clean up after your dog!

7.
When you visit temples or churches, it is important to wear formal clothes. This sign is from St. Peter's Basilica in the Vatican City. It means you can't wear vests, shorts or short skirts. You must wear long trousers or skirts.

C. *Write some rules or customs in Japan that you think are important for foreign visitors to know.*

SPEAK: Explaining rules and making suggestions

A. Rule expressions: *Match these expressions about rules and customs with the pictures below. Write the letter next to the expression.*

_____	You **can't** drink alcohol under 20 years of age.
_____	You **must** take off your shoes when entering someone's house.
_____	You **have to** score a goal to win!
_____	You **can** wear casual clothes.
_____	You **mustn't** use your phone when driving.
_____	You **don't have to** shake hands in Japan. You **can** bow.

B. Rules: *Write the letter of the rules or customs next to the questions below.*

_____	What is a Japanese custom when entering a house?
_____	What is one of the rules of soccer?
_____	What is a rule for driving?
_____	What is a Japanese custom when meeting someone for the first time?
_____	What is the dress code at university?
_____	What is a rule for drinking alcohol in Japan?

C. Let's talk! *In pairs, practice asking a question from part B, then your classmate provides a rule or suggestion from part A.*

Bonus: *Together, practice explaining rules to the following:*

● **What are the rules for this course?**

   You must ... You have to ... You mustn't ...

● **What are the rules when travelling on a train?**

   You mustn't ... You have to ... You can't ...

● **What are the rules in a library?**

   You can't ... You have to ... You mustn't ...

VOCABULARY

DL 33 · CD33

Adjectives		strongly A2	....	prohibition B1	....
absent B1	....	**Nouns**		rule A1	....
illegal A2	....	assignment B1	....	semester A2	....
late A1	....	custom A2	....	traffic A2 accident A2	....
legal B1	....	dress code +	....	**Verbs**	
private A2	....	experience A2	....	allow A2	....
public B1	....	garbage A1	....	belong A2	....
rude A1	....	homework A1	....	borrow A1	....
strict A1	....	jewelry A1	....	bow B2	....
Adverbs/Determiners/Pronouns		law A2	....	disturb A2	....
carefully A1	....	leisure A2	....	fail A2	....
early A1	....	life A1	....	follow A2	....
far A2	....	make-up A2	....	memorize B1	....
(a) few A2	....	mosque A2	....	pass A2	....
loudly A2	....	obligation B2	....	prohibit B2	....
most A1	....	permission A2	....	wake (up) B1	....
quietly A2	....	phone A1	....	warn B1	....

A. *Match each definition with the words on the right.*

1. Missing: _____

2. Free time: _____

3. Against the law: _____

4. Give permission to do something: _____

5. Spring or fall period at university: _____

a) semester

b) illegal

c) absent

d) allow

e) leisure

B. *Write a word from the vocabulary with the opposite meaning:*

1. public _____

2. pass _____

3. illegal _____

4. loudly _____

5. prohibit _____

C. Give your opinion!

1. It's rude to eat on a train.
   Agree: _____ Disagree: _____
   Why? _____

2. Smoking should be prohibited in all public places.
   Agree: _____ Disagree: _____
   Why? _____

3. There should be a strict dress code at university.
   Agree: _____ Disagree: _____
   Why? _____

4. Students should be allowed to use phones in class, if they ask permission.
   Agree: _____ Disagree: _____
   Why? _____

5. Students should be allowed to wear make-up at high school.
   Agree: _____ Disagree: _____
   Why? _____

GRAMMAR

Explaining laws, rules and customs using modal verbs in the present and past simple

Prohibition - present tense (mustn't, can't)	Prohibition - past tense (couldn't)
You mustn't be absent from class a lot.	*My sister couldn't wear make-up at high school.*
You can't park your car here.	*When I was a child, I couldn't stay up late.*
Obligation - present tense (must, have to)	**Obligation - past tense (had to)**
Do we have to buy a text book?	*She had to wear a uniform in high school.*
You must finish your assignment this week.	*My brother failed the test, so he had to take it again.*
No obligation - present tense (don't have to)	**No obligation - past tense (didn't have to)**
He doesn't have to wear a tie at work.	*I didn't have to make dinner last night. My friend cooked.*
I don't have to work tomorrow.	*They didn't have to get up early last Sunday.*
Permission- present tense (can)	**Permission- past tense (could)**
Can I go to the toilet, please?	*At school, I could use my phone after class, not during*
You can sit here.	*lessons.*

A. *Choose the modal verb that <u>best</u> completes the sentences below.*

1. You _____ drive over 100km/h on expressways in Japan. (have to / can't)

2. Yesterday, she _____ write two assignments. (had to / mustn't)

3. In Japan, you _____ drink alcohol if you are under 20. (can't / must)

4. When I was 15, I _____ go to bed early on weekends. (didn't have to / mustn't)

5. You _____ only smoke in special smoking areas. (mustn't / can)

6. She _____ put on a sweater this morning because it was cold. (had to / can)

7. You _____ tip in restaurants in Japan. (don't have to / have to)

B. *Match the questions with the answers.*

1. Do I have to turn off my phone in class? ____   a) Of course you can. Here you are.

2. Can I borrow your pen? ____   b) No, I didn't. I started at junior high school.

3. Could your sister go to the concert? ____   c) No, you don't, but use the silent mode.

4. Do I have to come to school tomorrow? ____   d) Yes. My mother gave her permission.

5. Did you have to study English at elementary school? ____   e) No, you don't. Tomorrow is a holiday.

C. *Match the sign with the rule.*

1.
_____   a) You have to stop.

2.
_____   b) You can't eat or drink here.

3.
_____   c) You mustn't take photographs here.

4.
_____   d) You can park here.

LISTEN

A. Pre-listening

1. *A university teacher is explaining the rules of his English class. Guess the missing words.*

2. *Listen and check your answers.*

 DL 34 CD34

> Welcome everyone to my English class. I want you to pass this course so please follow the class rules. Rule 1: Don't be absent. You must attend _____ of the classes to pass. This means you can only be absent _____ times. Rule 2: Try to speak English. You must speak English to me and to your classmates to _____ this course. Rule 3: You have to bring a _____ to class. You will learn lots of new _____ so a dictionary will be really _____. Follow these rules to help you pass this _____.

B. Discussion: *What's your opinion about this listening?*

What other rules are important for a language course?   *I think ...*

C. *Listen to two more announcements about rules. Choose the correct answer from a, b or c.*

Announcement 1    DL 35 CD35

1. According to the police officer, the number of traffic accidents is:
   a) Going up
   b) Going down
   c) Staying the same

2. What is the speed limit for driving on the highway?
   a) 100 km per hour
   b) Over 100 km per hour
   c) Under 50 km per hour

3. The word "fine" is closest in meaning to:
   a) Homework
   b) Penalty
   c) Letter

Announcement 2   DL 36 CD36

4. "Accident" is closest in meaning to:
   a) Injury
   b) Party
   c) Lesson

5. Why is running not allowed near the pool?
   a) Because the pool is crowded.
   b) Because the floor is not dry.
   c) Because the pool is noisy.

6. What was the last rule?
   a) You cannot dive in the pool.
   b) You cannot run near the pool.
   c) You cannot use the pool if you are unhealthy.

D. Post-listening: *With a partner, decide what rules you would like to have (or change) at university.*

COMMUNICATE

Culture Quiz – Rules of the World (Partner A)

Read the rules to your partner. Write your partner's guess (true or false) in the table.
Check your partner's score using the answers below.

	True or False
1. You are not allowed to bring chewing gum into Singapore.	
2. You mustn't touch people on the head in Thailand. It is very rude.	
3. In Mexico, you can't eat tacos with your hands. You must use a knife and fork.	
4. In South Korea, men have to do military service.	
5. It is illegal to feed pigeons on the streets of San Francisco.	
6. In New Zealand, you can't start driving until you are 21.	
7. People in India mustn't eat chicken. Chickens are holy animals for Hindus.	
8. In Spain, you can't drink alcohol if you are under the age of 21.	
9. You shouldn't flush the toilet after 10:00 p.m. in some apartment blocks in Switzerland.	
10. You have to drive on the left in Ireland.	
Total number of correct answers:	

ANSWERS: 1-true, 2-true, 3-false (you usually eat tacos with your hands), 4- true, 5-true, 6- false (you can start driving at 16), 7-false (but beef is banned as cows are holy animals), 8-false (the legal drinking age is 16), 9-true, 10-true

10 points	You are an expert on international cultures and customs. Perhaps you should become a diplomat in the future. Or maybe you cheated!
7-9 points	You know a lot about different rules and customs around the world. You are interested in learning about cultural differences.
4-6 points	Although you do know some things about the rules and customs of different countries, you should read more about different cultures.
1-3 points	There is more to the world than staying at home! You should open your eyes and learn more about the world around you.
0 points	Really?! Zero?! No points at all! I guess you don't like traveling!

Culture Quiz – Rules of the World (Partner B)

Read the rules to your partner. Write your partner's guess (true or false) in the table.
Check your partner's score using the answers below.

	True or False
1. Women are not allowed to join the army in Israel.	
2. In Australia, you don't have to tip in restaurants.	
3. You mustn't eat with your right hand in Indonesia. You should use your left hand.	
4. In Italy, you should drink cappuccino in the morning, not in the afternoon.	
5. In Sweden, you have to drive with your lights on even during the day.	
6. In China, you should give clocks or shoes as gifts at a wedding.	
7. Women have to cover their heads and arms when they enter a mosque in Egypt.	
8. You mustn't give the "OK" sign to someone in Brazil. It is very rude.	
9. In some historic places in Greece, such as the Acropolis, you can't wear high heels.	
10. You have to show your passport when traveling from England to Scotland.	
Total number of correct answers:	

ANSWERS: *1-false, 2-true, 3-false (It's rude to eat with your left hand), 4-true, 5-true, 6-false (they are bad luck), 7-true, 8-true, 9-true, 10- false (both England and Scotland are part of the UK)*

10 points	You are an expert on international cultures and customs. Perhaps you should become a diplomat in the future. Or maybe you cheated!
7-9 points	You know a lot about different rules and customs around the world. You are interested in learning about cultural differences.
4-6 points	Although you do know some things about the rules and customs of different countries, you should read more about different cultures.
1-3 points	There is more to the world than staying at home! You should open your eyes and learn more about the world around you.
0 points	Really?! Zero?! No points at all! I guess you don't like traveling!

A. Brainstorm

Do you agree, or not agree, with your school rules?

For example, taking tests, wearing a school uniform, using phones in class

I don't agree with ……… because …

B. Pre-reading

1. Write the high school and university rules next to the pictures from the table below.

2. Write two more rules for both high school and university in the spaces below.

At high school	At university

I couldn't wear make-up or jewelry.

I can wear casual clothes. I don't have to wear a uniform.

I couldn't use my phone in the classroom.

I have to cook my own dinner in the evening.

I had to wear a school uniform.

I have to do lots of homework and assignments.

We had to clean the school every evening before we went home.

I don't have to wake up so early every day.

High school rules vs University rules

C. *Read a student's experience of high school and university, then answer the following questions.* DL 37  CD37

> At my high school, there were many rules. I woke up at 6:00 a.m. every day because classes started between 8:00 – 8:30 a.m. I had to wear a school uniform. I didn't like my uniform because it was boring. Girls weren't allowed to wear make-up or jewelry. I had to take a bus to school because it was far from the train station. I could bring my phone to school, but I wasn't allowed to use it in class. At lunch, we all had to eat in the school cafeteria. I didn't like the meals because there wasn't much choice. Finally after school, I had to take extra English classes three times a week. I had to do a lot of homework to pass all the tests. High school was very tiring!
>
> At my university the rules are different. I like being a university student because I don't have to wake up early! My apartment is next to the university. I also don't have to wear a uniform. I love wearing casual clothes! My major is International Business. I have to attend lots of classes, and I mustn't be late for class. I have to get 60% to pass my English classes but I want to get over 80% so I can get an "A" grade! I can eat my lunch at the cafeteria, but I don't like the food there. I try to cook my own food, but I have no time because I have a part-time job. I work most evenings at a convenience store. I finish at 10:00 p.m. so I have no time to cook my dinner. I want to find a different part-time job so I have more free time.

1. What time did classes start at high school?
- **a)** 6:00 a.m.
- **b)** 9:30 a.m.
- **c)** After 8:30 a.m.
- **d)** From 8:00 a.m.

2. Why didn't the student like her school uniform?
- **a)** Because it was expensive.
- **b)** Because it was cheap.
- **c)** Because it wasn't interesting.
- **d)** All of the above.

3. What couldn't the student use in class?
- **a)** The bus
- **b)** Homework
- **c)** Her phone
- **d)** English

4. Why didn't the student like the school cafeteria food?
- **a)** It was always the same.
- **b)** She was tired.
- **c)** It was unhealthy.
- **d)** It was healthy.

5. According to the student, which of these is NOT true?
- **a)** She needs 60% to pass her English course.
- **b)** She can't cook because of her part-time job.
- **c)** She needs less than 80% for an "A" grade.
- **d)** She wants 80% or more for an "A" grade.

6. What do you know from this reading?
- **a)** The student liked high school more than university.
- **b)** The student prefers cooking to eating at university.
- **c)** The student doesn't like the uniform at university.
- **d)** The student enjoyed getting up early at high school.

WRITE

A. Word check: *Match the words in the vocabulary box below and fill in the gaps.*

At my high school, there were many rules. I _____ at 7:00 a.m. every day. I couldn't be _____ for class. I had to wear a uniform. There were tests every week. I had to study a lot of English. For example, I had to _____ lots of new words every week! I also couldn't use my _____ in class. My teacher was very _____ . We always had to follow her _____ .

At my _____ the rules are different. I don't have to wear a uniform, I can wear _____ clothes! I have to attend lots of classes. I only have _____ tests during the semester, but I also have a lot of writing _____ , and there are lots of tests at the end of the semester. I _____ to a tennis club. We play tennis twice a week. I also have a part-time job. I work in a convenience store during the week until 10:00 p.m., but I can go home _____ on Tuesdays.

belong	a few	casual	rules	memorize	late
phone	assignments	woke up	university	early	strict

B. Grammar check: *Practice writing rules using modal verbs (in the past and present) that best match the sentences below.*

1. I _____ be absent from too many classes. (can / mustn't)

2. I _____ wear make-up in school. (have to / couldn't)

3. I _____ get 80% or more to get an "A" grade. (have to / could)

4. I _____ eat food in the classroom. (can't / must)

5. I _____ speak in English as much as possible in class. (must / don't have to)

6. I _____ be late for class when I was at high school. (couldn't / didn't have to)

7. I _____ get up early on Sunday. I can stay in bed late. (mustn't / don't have to)

C. Writing skill: *Narrative paragraph writing*

Narrative writing is about writing a story. The story could be about things that have happened to you over time. For example: writing about your high school days.

● A narrative paragraph starts with a topic sentence followed by supporting details.
  For example: *I really like university life. I don't have to wake up early every day!*
● A narrative can be about you so make sure to use "I / my …"

Let's practice!

Write about the dress code at your high school and university.

At my high school _____

I _____

At my university _____

I _____

Task: *Are the rules at your high school and university similar or different?*

Write two paragraphs. Think of topics to write about, for example:

● Dress code

● Classes / English study

● Eating food

● Club activities

For example:

Paragraph 1: Write about the rules at your high school (use the past tense).

Paragraph 2: Write about the rules at your university (use the present tense).

Check the Reading on page 95 as a guide but use your <u>own</u> ideas! Remember to use a main idea and supporting details for each paragraph.

★ *Use the space below to plan your writing.*

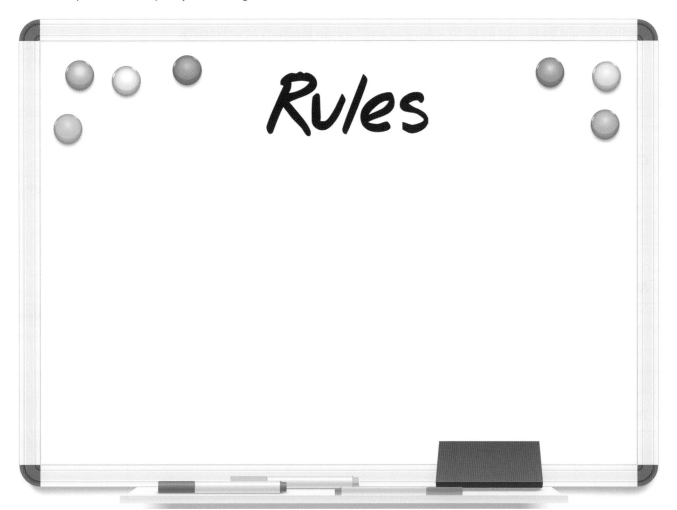

PROJECT

A. Question: *What rules are important for a Japanese university?*
Ask 10 university students their opinion about the following rules:

1. All students must study English.

	Strongly agree	Agree	Depends	Disagree	Strongly disagree
No.					
%					

2. All class sizes must be small (max 20 students per class).

	Strongly agree	Agree	Depends	Disagree	Strongly disagree
No.					
%					

3. All students must study a language in a foreign country for three months.

	Strongly agree	Agree	Depends	Disagree	Strongly disagree
No.					
%					

4. English should be taught by both Japanese and foreign teachers at university.

	Strongly agree	Agree	Depends	Disagree	Strongly disagree
No.					
%					

5. Classes should have Japanese and foreign students studying together.

	Strongly agree	Agree	Depends	Disagree	Strongly disagree
No.					
%					

6. All classrooms must have computers or students must use tablets.

	Strongly agree	Agree	Depends	Disagree	Strongly disagree
No.					
%					

7. The cafeteria must serve healthy Japanese and international food for students.

	Strongly agree	Agree	Depends	Disagree	Strongly disagree
No.					
%					

B. Results: *Choose pie charts (Module 1) or column charts (Module 2) to show your data.*

1. **All students must study English.**

2. **All class sizes must be small.**

3. **Students must study a language in a foreign country for three months.**

4. **English should be taught by both Japanese and foreign teachers at university.**

5. **Classes should have Japanese and foreign students studying together.**

6. **All classrooms must have computers or students must use tablets.**

7. **The cafeteria must serve healthy Japanese and international food for students.**

C. Report: *Write the results of your survey and think of reasons.*

For example: *80% of students strongly agree that all students must study English. Students must study English because it is the world language.*

_____

_____

_____

_____

_____

D. Presentation: *In groups, present your results to your classmates.*

CROSSWORD

Across

1. My mother is so _____. We have lots of rules at home.

4.

6. I have to do a lot of writing _____ for homework.

7. We don't have a _____ at university. We can wear casual clothes.

11.

15. I _____ my driving test last week. I'm very happy.

16.

17.

18.

19. You must study hard or you'll_____ the English test.

Down

2.

3. I _____ to the volleyball club at high school.

5.

6. I was _____ from school, because I had a cold.

8. We have two _____ at university, spring and fall.

9. Did you go to a public or _____ high school?

10. I always _____ at 6:30 a.m. in the morning.

12. You are not _____ to run in the swimming pool.

13.

14. In Japan, it is _____ to drink alcohol unless you are over 20.

MODULE 7

CULTURE

Can you scan for information about famous places in Japan?

Can you make recommendations for places to visit in Japan?

Can you understand culture vocabulary?

Can you ask questions about future plans and give recommendations?

Can you understand conversations about future plans?

Can you answer general knowledge culture questions?

Can you read and understand tourism advertisements?

Can you write an advertisement about a place you know well?

Can you find out Japan's tourist attractions from your classmates?

UNIT 13

MATCH

1.

6.

2.

5.

4.

3.

★ *Look at the pictures above. Try to guess which place or event matches each prefecture below. Write the letter of the prefecture in the space next to the picture above.*

A

B

C

D

E

F

SCAN: Name the famous sightseeing places in Japan

A. Scanning for information: *In **4 minutes**, quickly read the information below to find key words.*

B. *Write the names of the places or events under the correct picture on page 102. Write the name of each prefecture below the character and map.*   ⬇ DL 38   ⊙ CD 38

1. This is one of the most well-known hot spring resorts in Japan, and it is my favorite place in Kyushu. The natural hot baths are so relaxing and refreshing. There are also lots of different hell pools or "jigoku." The "Blood Pond Hell" is the most impressive. The water is bright red. If you like hot springs, I recommend visiting Beppu in Oita prefecture.

2.  With awesome ski resorts and breathtaking natural beauty, Nagano prefecture is an ideal place for skiing and snowboarding. The 1998 Winter Olympics took place in Hakuba in Nagano. Hakuba has some of the highest snowfall in Japan. It is a traditional town with excellent local food and lively nightlife. You must go!

3. For anyone interested in traditional Japanese culture, Itsukushima Shrine is a must-see. It is one of two UNESCO World Heritage Sites in Hiroshima prefecture, and the views of the floating torii gate are spectacular. Wild deer walk freely around Miyajima Island, and a cable car takes you to the top of Mt. Misen. It is one of the most scenic places in Japan!

4.  Himeji Castle is one of Japan's 12 original castles and one of the most historic places in Japan. Many people think Himeji Castle is the most beautiful in Japan. It is also a very popular cherry blossom viewing spot in spring, and can be very crowded in the Golden Week holiday period. If you can avoid busy days, a trip to this stunning castle in Hyogo prefecture will be an unforgettable experience.

5. Miyako Island is in the southernmost part of Japan, Okinawa prefecture. It has beautiful white sandy beaches, clear, blue water and coral reefs that are perfect for snorkeling and diving. The climate is mild and comfortable. Goya chanpuru is the most famous local dish. If you are into marine sports or like relaxing on a beach, this is definitely the place for you.

6.  There are summer festivals held in various parts of Aomori prefecture. The largest festival is the Nebuta Festival in Aomori city. The parades have huge, colorful floats and traditional singing and dancing. It is a lot of fun, and everyone wears traditional Haneto costumes. The food is delicious too. There are lots of places selling fresh seafood. In my opinion, it is the most exciting festival in Japan.

C. *Write about your favorite place in Japan.*

SPEAK: Making recommendations

A. Planning expressions: *Match these expressions with the pictures below:*

_____ **I'm thinking of** going surfing next weekend.

_____ **I'm planning to** go to a fireworks festival in August.

_____ **I'd like to** go camping this summer.

_____ **I want to** go hiking on my day off.

_____ **I'm going** shopping in Osaka next week.

_____ **I might** go sightseeing in Tokyo during Golden Week.

B. Giving recommendations: *Match the recommendations with the correct expressions above.*

_____ **If I were you, I'd** go to Lake Biwa fireworks festival. It's awesome!

_____ **You should** climb the mountain near my hometown. The view is beautiful.

_____ **You must** go to the night market in Dotonbori. You can buy great souvenirs there.

_____ **Check out** this camping website — it recommends lots of good camp sites.

_____ **You've got to** see the Kaminarimon in Asakusa!

_____ **Why don't you** go to Enoshima? I think it's the best place for surfing.

C. Let's talk!

1. In pairs, make plans using the expressions from part A, then your partner gives recommendations from part B.
2. Make plans to take a trip somewhere in Japan. Use the expressions **in bold** from part A.
   Your partner then gives their **own** recommendations.

For example:

    A: *I'm planning to* … *go to Kyoto next month.*

    B: *Really?* **If I were you**, *I'd* … *see the Kinkaku-ji Temple! I think it's the most beautiful temple in Japan!*

VOCABULARY

⬇ DL 39   ◉ CD39

Adjectives		modern ᴬ²		festival ᴬ¹	
authentic ⁺		perfect ᴬ²		fireworks ᴮ¹	
awesome ᴮ¹		pristine ⁺		hot spring ⁺	
beautiful ᴬ¹		refreshing ⁺		museum ᴬ²	
breathtaking ᴮ²		relaxing ᴮ¹		must ⁺	
crowded ᴬ²		scenic ᴮ¹		nature ᴬ²	
excellent ᴬ¹		traditional ᴬ²		nightlife ᴮ¹	
historic ᴮ¹		well-known ᴬ²		season ᴮ¹	
huge ᴮ¹		**Nouns**		specialty ᴮ²	
impressive ᴮ¹		atmosphere ᴮ¹		**Verbs**	
incredible ᴮ¹		building ᴬ¹		check out ⁺	
interesting ᴬ¹		cherry ᴮ² blossom ᴮ²		plan ᴮ¹	
lively ᴬ²		choice ᴬ²		recommend ᴮ¹	

A. *Match each definition with the words on the right.*

1. No room to move: _____

2. Looks good: _____

3. Has a beautiful view: _____

4. A famous place, person or thing: _____

a) well-known
b) scenic
c) impressive
d) crowded

B. *Choose a word from the box and complete each sentence.*

> breathtaking   nightlife   pristine   specialty

1. This restaurant is great. The beef is a _____.

2. They clean the rooms really well every day. They look _____!

3. There are no restaurants or bars. The _____ is terrible.

4. The view from the top of this building is _____.

C. Give your opinion!

1. Traditional Japanese music is relaxing.
   Agree: _____   Disagree: _____
   Why? _____

2. Spring is the best season in Japan.
   Agree: _____   Disagree: _____
   Why? _____

3. Going to a hot spring is the perfect way to relax.
   Agree: _____   Disagree: _____
   Why? _____

4. My hometown has a lot of nightlife.
   Agree: _____   Disagree: _____
   Why? _____

5. Japan is a modern country.
   Agree: _____   Disagree: _____
   Why? _____

6. Be sure to check out a summer fireworks festival. The atmosphere is awesome!
   Agree: _____   Disagree: _____
   Why? _____

GRAMMAR

Asking and answering questions about the future, and giving recommendations about the future.

"Wh" questions and answers (going to / planning to)	
Where are you going next month?	I'm going to Tokyo.
When is he going to visit Kyushu?	He's going to visit next week.
Who is he going on holiday with?	He's going with friends.
What are you planning to do tommorow?	I'm going shopping.
Yes/No questions (going to / planning to)	
Are you going to Spain next year?	Yes, I am. I'm going to Madrid.
Are you going to take the train to school?	No, I'm not. I'm going to take the bus.
Is she planning to go to Osaka next week?	No, she isn't. She's going next month.

A. *Change the verbs into the correct future form using "going to" or "planning to".*

1. What (you / do) _____ next summer?

2. When (you / meet) _____ your high school friends?

3. Where (you / eat) _____ lunch tomorrow?

4. _____ (you / travel) _____ abroad next year?

5. _____ (you and your friends / go) _____ shopping this weekend?

★ *Now ask your partner the questions from part A.*

B. *Change the verbs into the correct future form using "going to" or "planning to".*

1. My sister (study) _____ Art at university next year.

2. My friends (watch) _____ a movie tonight.

3. I (visit) _____ my grandparents in the New Year vacation.

"If" + simple present + main clause
If you go to Tokyo, you should see the palace.
If you come to my hometown, you should eat sushi.
If you go to Okinawa, you'll love the beaches.
If your friend is into Japanese culture, she'll enjoy going to Kyoto.

C. *Arrange the words in correct order.*

1. nightlife / like / you / if / should / you / city / to / go / the

_____

2. culture / see / you / if / want / to / museum / you / go / a / should / to

_____

3. Utsunomiya / into / you'll / gyoza / you / love / if / are

_____

LISTEN

A. Pre-listening

1. Read the conversation between students planning a trip in Japan. Guess the missing words.

2. Listen to the conversation, check your answers and complete the conversation.   DL 40   CD40

Hey Aimi, I'm going to visit a friend in Oita next month, and she's taking me to Beppu to enjoy the _____. Have you been there?

Yes, I have. I went to Beppu last year with my _____.

Great. Can you _____ any good hot springs?

Well, there are so many different types. We went to one on top of a _____. The view was _____.

Great! I love taking trips to the _____ to relax.

Yeah, Beppu is nice, but for me, I like going to the city to have fun. I love _____ and nightlife. I love the _____ of crowded cities!

B. Discussion: *What do you think about this conversation?*

For example:

"I like going to the city to have fun."   *I agree with Aimi. I think ...*

C. *Listen to different people recommending a trip to their hometown. Choose the correct answer from a, b or c.*

Recommendation 1   DL 41   CD41   **Recommendation 2**   DL 42   CD42

1. How does the man describe the view of the cherry blossoms?

   a) Beautiful   **b)** Scenic   **c)** Bright

4. What is special about the amusement park's roller-coaster?

   a) It is the fastest in the prefecture.

   b) It is the longest in the prefecture.

   c) It is the tallest in the prefecture.

2. When does the man enjoy seeing the castle the most?

   a) Cherry blossom season

   b) End of March

   c) Winter

5. What percent discount does a friend receive?

   a) 4%   **b)** 50%   **c)** 15%

3. Why should people see Kengun Shrine?

   a) It's covered in snow.

   b) It's the oldest shrine in the city.

   c) It's the oldest castle in the city.

6. What is popular for children at Amigo's?

   a) Ice cream

   b) Coffee

   c) Discount prices

D. Post-listening: *With a partner, decide the best place to go on vacation in Japan.*

CONNECT 5

PLAYER A

PLAYER B

Connect 5 rules:

1. Toss a coin, the winner is Player A. Player A moves down (top to bottom) and Player B moves across (left to right).

2. Player A chooses a hexagon from the top row. Player B asks a question matching the shape (star, diamond, heart or triangle) on page 109. If you can answer the question, color in the hexagon.

3. Player B then chooses a hexagon from the left side. Player A asks a question matching the shape on page 109. If you choose a diamond hexagon, guess the word shown in the picture.

4. Each player then chooses any hexagon next to their colored one. Their partner then asks a question or they guess the word in the picture.

5. The player that connects a line of hexagons from top to bottom, or left to right, wins.

CONNECT 5
QUESTIONS

★ STAR	▲ TRIANGLE	♥ HEART	◆ DIAMOND
What are you going to do next weekend?	Where do you recommend visiting if you are interested in Japanese culture?	What is the longest river in the world?	
Where are you planning to go this summer?	What city should you go to if you like lively nightlife?	Which is bigger, the Atlantic Ocean or the Indian Ocean?	
Are you going abroad next year?	What will you do this weekend if it rains?	Hokkaido is the largest prefecture in Japan. What is the second largest?	
Are you going to do anything interesting next weekend?	Complete the sentence: If you like animation, you'll love …	Which foreign country would you most like to visit?	
What are you going to eat tonight?	Complete the sentence: If I can save money next year, …	Lake Tazawa is the deepest lake in Japan. Where is it?	
Are you going to study English tomorrow?	Complete the sentence: If I lose my smartphone, …	In which country is the oldest university in the world?	
Who are you going to meet after class?	Complete the sentence: If I study abroad next year, …	Which prefecture do you think has the most delicious food in Japan?	

WRITE YOUR OWN QUESTIONS

?	?	?	?

A. Brainstorm

In pairs, discuss what you know about Hokkaido.

For example: *places, weather, food, things to do.*

What recommendations can you give to tourists?

B. Pre-reading *Read the expressions in part A below (A-F). Try to complete the expressions without looking at part B. Then, match the expressions in part A with part B.*

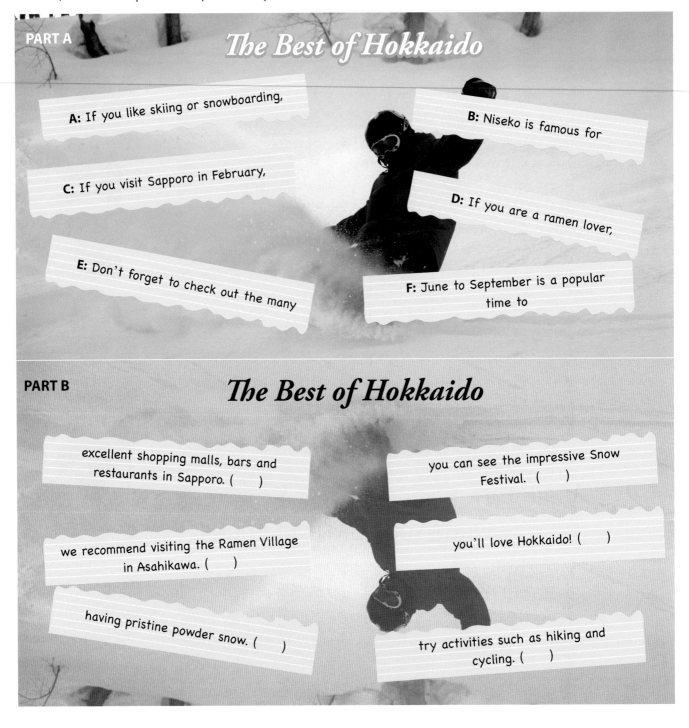

PART A

The Best of Hokkaido

A: If you like skiing or snowboarding,

B: Niseko is famous for

C: If you visit Sapporo in February,

D: If you are a ramen lover,

E: Don't forget to check out the many

F: June to September is a popular time to

PART B

The Best of Hokkaido

excellent shopping malls, bars and restaurants in Sapporo. (　　)

you can see the impressive Snow Festival. (　　)

we recommend visiting the Ramen Village in Asahikawa. (　　)

you'll love Hokkaido! (　　)

having pristine powder snow. (　　)

try activities such as hiking and cycling. (　　)

C. *Read a tourism advertisement about Hokkaido, then answer the following questions.*   DL 43   CD43

The Best of Hokkaido

Incredible natural beauty as well as perfect snow conditions, if you like nature or skiing and snowboarding, you'll love Hokkaido! Come to visit in winter, and be sure to check out Niseko. It's one of the most famous ski resorts in Japan. Niseko is really popular with foreigners such as Chinese, Americans, Canadians and especially Australians. Niseko is famous for having pristine powder snow, which makes it a great place for skiing. There are lots of different ski resorts to check out, and seeing the breathtaking Mount Yotei is a must!

You should also visit Sapporo: the capital of Hokkaido. If you visit Sapporo in February, you can see one of the most impressive winter events in Japan: the snow festival! More than two million people see this event each year. Also, if you like entertainment, don't forget to check out the many, excellent shopping malls, restaurants and bars that Sapporo has to offer.

Summer in Hokkaido is also fantastic. Hokkaido is cooler than other parts of Japan, which means it's ideal for camping. June to September is a popular time to enjoy the outdoors, and try activities such as hiking and cycling. The weather at this time of year is perfect, and Hokkaido's scenery is amazing.

As for food, treat yourself to Hokkaido's excellent seafood. If you have time, try visiting one of the many popular seafood markets. In addition, be sure to sample Hokkaido's other food specialty: ramen! If you are a ramen lover, we recommend visiting the Ramen Village in Asahikawa. It has a variety of dishes to choose from.

1. Which foreigners visit Niseko the most?
 a) Chinese
 b) Americans
 c) Australians
 d) Canadians

2. What does "powder" snow mean?
 a) The snow is heavy for skiing.
 b) The snow is good for skiing.
 c) The snow is cheap for skiing.
 d) The snow is icy for skiing.

3. "Two million" in paragraph 2 means:
 a) 2,000
 b) 200,000
 c) 20,000,000
 d) 2,000,000

4. According to the reading, when is the best time to go camping?
 a) Spring
 b) Fall
 c) Summer
 d) February

5. The word "variety" in paragraph 4 is closest in meaning to:
 a) A few
 b) Many
 c) Same
 d) Anytime

6. What do you know from this reading?
 a) Winter is the best time to see Hokkaido.
 b) Summer is the best time to see Hokkaido.
 c) Ramen is more popular than seafood.
 d) People should visit in summer and winter.

A. Word check: *Complete this advertisement about Tokyo. Use words from the vocabulary box below to help you.*

The Best of Tokyo

___Excellent___ shops and restaurants, and _____ nightlife, if you like shopping and eating out, you'll love Tokyo! Come to visit in spring, and be sure to check out the _____ cherry blossom in Ueno Park. It is also a great place to have a _____ picnic. I recommend going to the top of the Skytree. The views are _____. If you have time, try visiting Meiji Jingu Shrine. It is one of the most _____ places in Tokyo.

Going to a fireworks festival is also a _____. August is a _____ time to enjoy fireworks festivals. Sumidagawa Fireworks Festival is one of the most _____ in Japan. But be careful, the weather at this time of year is very _____ and _____.

As for food, treat yourself to unagi. This is barbecued eel and is really _____. It gives you energy in the summer. Finally, be sure to check out the fish at Tsukiji Outer Market. If you are a seafood _____, we recommend learning to make sushi.

perfect	impressive	awesome	relaxing	traditional	~~excellent~~
beautiful	humid	hot	breathtaking	delicious	lover	must

B. Grammar check: *Practice giving recommendations using If + simple present + main clauses.*

If you like nature, you'll love _____

If you are a beach lover, I recommend visiting _____

August is a popular time to _____

If you visit my hometown in April, you can _____

My hometown is famous for _____

In winter, you should _____

C. Writing skill: *Persuasive writing*

Persuasive writing is about making the reader agree something. For example:

You should eat vegetables / **be sure to** go to bed early.

Provide reasons and adjectives to make the reader agree to something. For example:

*This restaurant is **excellent** because it has a great **atmosphere**.*

*If you like surfing, **be sure to** check out Kugenuma beach. The waves are **awesome**!*

Also, use superlatives to support your ideas. For example:

*Niseko is **one of the most famous** ski resorts in Japan.*

Let's practice!

Complete a tourism advertisement about Tokyo. Use the examples from page 112 but write your own ideas! Also, use words from the Vocabulary page to help you.

If you like _____, you'll love _____

It's a great place to _____

If you visit Tokyo in _____, be sure to check out

_____

Tokyo is one of the best cities for _____

_____ is famous for _____

Task: *Write a tourism advertisement about your home town or a place you know well. Use words from the Vocabulary page and expressions from the Speak page to help you.*

Write 2/3 short paragraphs about different topics, for example:

Paragraph 1: Introduction

Paragraph 2: Things to do in the spring / summer / fall / winter

Paragraph 3: Food

★ *Use the space below to plan your writing.*

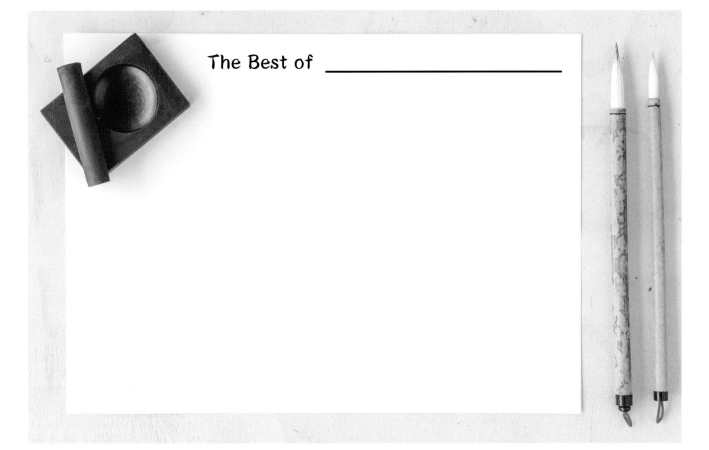

The Best of _____

PROJECT

A. Question: *What are Japan's best tourist attractions?*

Ask 10 students the questions in the table below about Japan. Think of two more questions and write them in the boxes. Use words from the Vocabulary and Speak pages to help you. For example, "What is the most beautiful beach in Japan?"

Find out reasons for students' answers.

Interviews

	1. What is the most beautiful prefecture in Japan? Why?	2. Where are the most relaxing hot springs in Japan? Why?	3. What is the most historic building in Japan? Why?	4.	5.
1					
2					
3					
4					
5					
6					
7					
8					
9					
10					
Results					

B. Report: *Write about any similarities or differences in your results. Try to use main ideas and supporting details.*

For example:

From my results, the most beautiful prefecture in Japan is Nagano. Four students said the scenery is amazing.

C. Presentation: *What are Japan's best attractions?*

Part 1: Use your results from part B and make notes giving recommendations about Japan. Use the Vocabulary and Speak pages to help you.

For example:

You should go to Nagano prefecture because the scenery is amazing. And you must also visit Beppu in Oita prefecture. The hot springs are so relaxing!

Presentation tip: Use B4/A3 paper, draw images of your results and use them in your presentation.

CROSSWORD

Across

3. Some parts of Tokyo are old and historic, but others are new and ____.

4.

7.

8.

9.

11. Niseko's powder snow is ____ for snowboarding.

13. You should go to Hakodate, because the night view is ____.

16.

17. I don't like quiet towns. I like big, ____ cities.

18.

Down

1. I love staying at five-star hotels, they are so ____.

2. If you like ____ buildings, you'll love Kyoto.

3. The Louvre is the most famous ____ in Paris.

5. It is a difficult ____ whether to go to the beach or the mountains.

6.

7.

10. Osaka has lots of bars and restaurants. It's famous for its ____.

12. If you are into Chinese food, I ____ Yokohama Chinatown.

14. The pizza at that restaurant is really ____. It is the same as I ate in Italy.

15.

Framework English

2020年 1 月20日　初版第 1 刷発行
2022年 2 月20日　初版第 4 刷発行

著　者　Colin Thompson
　　　　Tim Woolstencroft

発行者　福　岡　正　人
発行所　株式会社　金　星　堂

（〒101-0051）東京都千代田区神田神保町 3-21
Tel　（03）3263-3828（営業部）
　　　（03）3263-3997（編集部）
Fax　（03）3263-0716
http://www.kinsei-do.co.jp

編集担当　松本　明子　　　　　　　Printed in Japan
印刷所・製本所／倉敷印刷株式会社
ISBN978-4-7647-4107-2　C1082

MODULE 1: LANGUAGE REVIEW

A. *Put the questions in the correct order and answer them.*

1. music / like / you / do / what / ?

    Q. _____

    A. _____

2. major / your / is / what / ?

    Q. _____

    A. _____

3. the / you / near / live / do / university / ?

    Q. _____

    A. _____

4. from / teacher / is / your / Japan / ?

    Q. _____

    A. _____

5. you / sports / play / what / do / ?

    Q. _____

    A. _____

B. *Match the questions and answers.*

1. Do you like ice cream? _____
2. Is he from Kyushu? _____
3. Do they speak English? _____
4. Does she work in Chiba? _____
5. Is he married? _____
6. Is her birthday in December? _____
7. Are you a Business major? _____

a) Yes, they do. They study English twice a week.
b) No, he isn't. He is single.
c) Yes, I am. I want to work for a bank after I graduate.
d) Yes, it is. Her birthday is on Christmas Day.
e) No, he isn't. He's from Shikoku.
f) No, she doesn't. She works in Saitama.
g) Yes, I do. I love vanilla.

C. *Choose the correct word and complete each sentence.*

1. Dancing is my favorite _____.   a) university   b) hobby   c) meal
2. I like hanging out with friends in my _____.   a) free time   b) interests   c) job
3. Studying abroad in another _____ sounds exciting!   a) country   b) city   c) prefecture
4. For homework, you have to _____ to find information.   a) major   b) be into   c) go online

D. *Choose the correct word from the box that best completes the questions. Answer the questions.*

fun	do	from	blood	into

1. What do you _____?   A: _____
2. What is your _____ type?   A: _____
3. What do you do for _____?   A: _____
4. Where are you _____?   A: _____
5. Are you _____ horror movies?   A: _____

119

MODULE 1: SELF-CHECK

A: *Write notes, words or expressions in the boxes to show what you have learned from this module.*

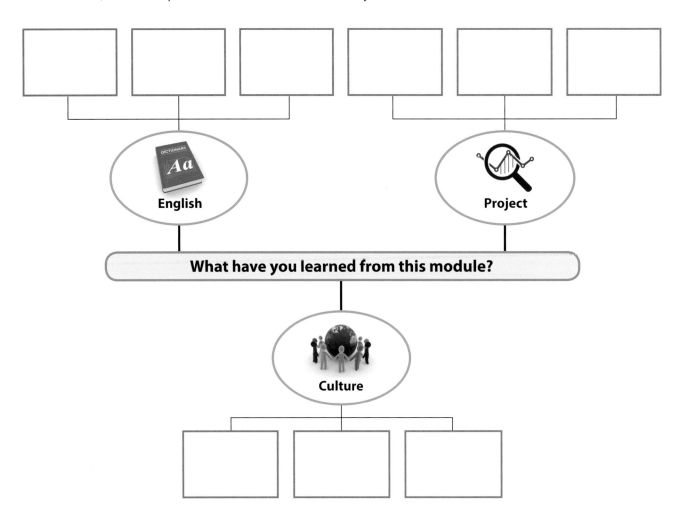

B: *Write a score (1-5)* in the boxes below to show how well you can do each part of the module. If you can't do any part well, go back to the page and practice again.*

Scan:	I can scan for information from introductions (p. 7).	☐
Speak:	I can introduce myself and ask personal questions (p. 8).	☐
Vocabulary:	I can understand introduction vocabulary (p. 9).	☐
Grammar:	I can ask "Wh" and Yes/No personal questions and give answers (p . 10).	☐
Listen:	I can understand people when they introduce themselves (p.11).	☐
Communicate:	I can ask and answer personal questions about other people (p. 12-13).	☐
Read:	I can read and understand introduction messages (p. 15).	☐
Write:	I can write an email introducing myself (p. 17).	☐
Project:	I can find out personal information about my classmates (p. 18).	☐
	I can present data using pie charts (p. 19).	☐

*(1="Not at all", 2="A little", 3="OK", 4="Well", 5="Very well")

Student ID: _____   Name: _____

MODULE 2: LANGUAGE REVIEW

A. *Put the questions in the correct order and answer them.*

1. friends / out / eat / your / with / you / do / ?

    Q. _____

    A. _____

2. lunch / do / what / usually / for / eat / you / ?

    Q. _____

    A. _____

3. you / what / food / kind / do / of / eat / often / ?

    Q. _____

    A. _____

B. *Put the words in the correct order.*

1. spicy / food / love / I / because / like / curry / I / .

_____

2. Neapolitan spaghetti / often / I / because / tomato / sauce / like / I / eat / .

_____

C. *Match the questions and answers.*

1. Do your parents like sushi? _____   **a)** Yes they do. They love tuna and salmon.

2. What desserts does your brother like? _____   **b)** He likes ice cream.

3. What do you usually drink in the morning? _____   **c)** I always drink coffee. I love lattes.

4. What restaurant do you often go to? _____   **d)** I usually go to the Chinese place near my apartment.

D. *Choose the correct word and complete each sentence.*

1. If I get up late in the morning, I sometimes skip _____.

    a) breakfast   **b)** dinner   **c)** dessert

2. The meal is three courses. There is a starter, a main course and a _____.

    a) lunch   **b)** meal   **c)** dessert

3. I usually go to the sushi restaurant near my apartment. The _____ is so fresh.

    a) fish   **b)** meat   **c)** fruit

4. I like this restaurant _____ the food is cheap but healthy.

    a) never   **b)** so   **c)** because

E. *Choose the correct word from the box that best completes the questions. Answer the questions.*

vegetables	fried	sour	time	cooking

1. Do you often eat deep _____ food?   A: _____

2. Do you like _____ fruit?   A: _____

3. What _____ do you never eat?   A: _____

4. What are you good at _____?   A: _____

5. What _____ do you usually eat dinner?   A: _____

MODULE 2: SELF-CHECK

A: *Write notes, words or expressions in the boxes to show what you have learned from this module.*

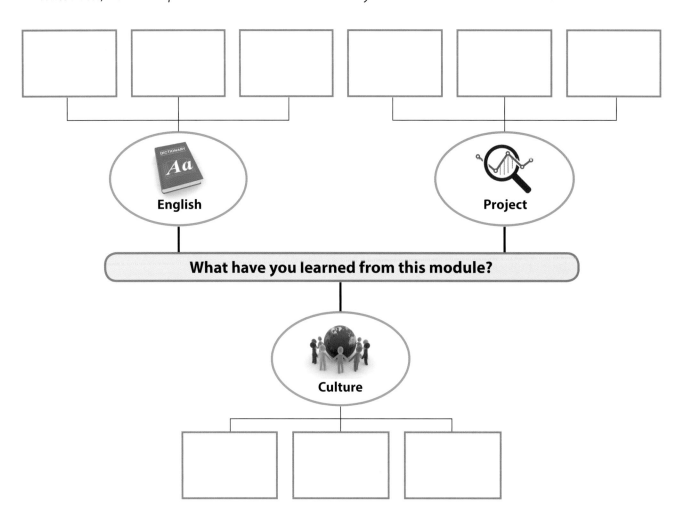

B: *Write a score (1-5)* in the boxes below to show how well you can do each part of the module. If you can't do any part well, go back to the page and practice again.*

Scan: I can scan for information about food from different countries (p. 23). ☐

Speak: I can talk about my eating habits (p. 24). ☐

Vocabulary: I can understand food vocabulary (p. 25). ☐

Grammar: I can use adverbs of frequency to discuss eating habits (p. 26). ☐

Listen: I can understand a conversation about eating habits (p.27). ☐

Communicate: I can ask and answer questions about food and drink (p. 28). ☐

Read: I can read and understand restaurant menus and restaurant reviews (p. 29-30). ☐

Write: I can write a restaurant review (p. 33). ☐

Project: I can find out the eating habits of my classmates (p. 34). ☐

                 I can present data using column charts (p. 35). ☐

*(1="Not at all", 2="A little", 3="OK", 4="Well", 5="Very well")

Student ID: _____   Name: _____

122

MODULE 3: LANGUAGE REVIEW

A. *Put the words in the correct order.*

1. parents / stand / can't / with / I / shopping / my /. _____

2. I'm / dyeing / my / hair / into / really /. _____

3. than / more / shoes / formal / I / sneakers / like /. _____

4. wearing / I / like / sweaters / wool /. _____

B. *Match the questions and answers.*

1. Does your father like wearing a suit? ____

2. Does your friend like tattoos? ____

3. Are you into wearing bright colors? ____

4. Does your sister like designer bags? ____

a) Yes, she does. She loves stylish brands.

b) Yes, he does. He thinks they look cool.

c) No, he doesn't. He prefers casual clothes.

d) No, I'm not. I like dark clothes.

C. *Put the questions in the correct order and answer them.*

1. striped / t-shirts / like / do / you / ?

Q. _____

A. _____

2. you / think / do / cool /are / beards / ?

Q. _____

A. _____

3. you / wearing / are / what / ?

Q. _____

A. _____

D. *Choose the correct word and complete each sentence.*

1. I've never seen this design. It's really _____.   **a)** uniform   **b)** unique   **c)** latest

2. It's my university graduation tomorrow so I have to wear a _____ suit.

a) formal   **b)** latest   **c)** cold

3. He doesn't like to shave. That's why he has a _____.   **a)** special offer   **b)** design   **c)** beard

4. I don't like plain t-shirts. I prefer _____ ones.   **a)** sale   **b)** striped   **c)** earring

E. *Choose the correct word from the box that best completes the questions. Answer the questions.*

wearing	think	sneakers	enjoy	interested

1. Are you _____ in fashion?   A: _____

2. What do you _____ of uniforms?   A: _____

3. Do you like _____ loose clothes?   A: _____

4. Is your classmate wearing _____?   A: _____

5. Do you _____ shopping for clothes?   A: _____

123

MODULE 3: SELF-CHECK

A: *Write notes, words or expressions in the boxes to show what you have learned from this module.*

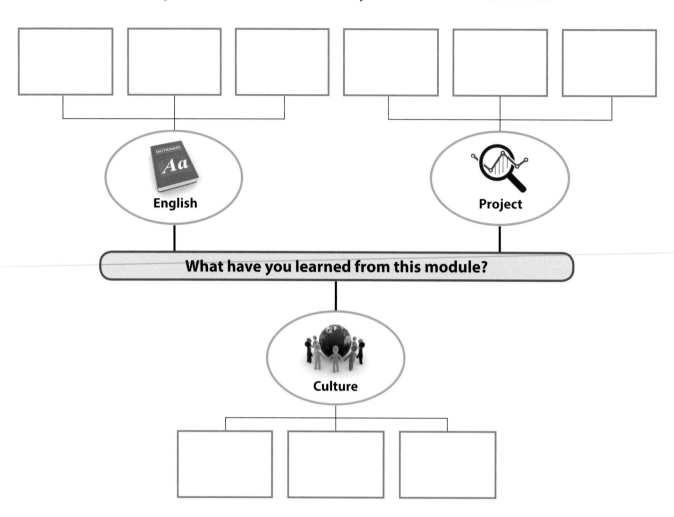

B: *Write a score (1-5)* in the boxes below to show how well you can do each part of the module. If you can't do any part well, go back to the page and practice again.*

Scan:	I can scan for information about fashion styles (p. 39).	☐
Speak:	I can talk about my fashion interests (p. 40).	☐
Vocabulary:	I can understand fashion vocabulary (p. 41).	☐
Grammar:	I can express likes and dislikes when discussing fashion (p. 42).	☐
Listen:	I can understand a conversation about fashion (p.43).	☐
Communicate:	I can find out about my classmates' fashion styles (p. 44).	☐
Read:	I can read and understand people's opinions about fashion (p. 45-46).	☐
Write:	I can write my opinion about the clothes I like (p. 49).	☐
Project:	I can find out my classmates opinions about fashion (p. 50).	☐
	I can present data using Likert scales and line charts (p. 51).	☐

*(1="Not at all", 2="A little", 3="OK", 4="Well", 5="Very well")

Student ID: _____   Name: _____

MODULE 4: LANGUAGE REVIEW

A. *Choose the correct word and complete each sentence.*

1. You should _____ medicine.

   a) do   **b)** drink   **c)** take

2. You should _____ home.

   a) play   **b)** stay   **c)** live

3. I _____ to a dentist twice a year.

   a) am   **b)** does   **c)** go

4. I feel sick. I need to go to the _____.

   a) addict   **b)** sleep   **c)** doctor

5. I love going to the gym. I _____ three times a week.

   a) exercise   **b)** positive   **c)** excited

6. You look really _____. Try to relax and don't worry so much!

   a) stressed   **b)** positive   **c)** excited

B. *Put the words in the correct order.*

1. exercises / twice / week / a / my friend / .   _____

2. tennis / plays / my father / three / a / times / week / .   _____

3. sushi / once / eat / I / week / a / .   _____

4. rarely / sleep / more / than / hours / 6 / I / day / a / . _____

5. I / take / should / medicine / often / how / ? _____

6. often / your brother / does / fast food / eat / how / ? _____

C. *Match the health problems and advice.*

1. I want to get fit. _____   **A.** Try to wear a mask when you go outside.

2. I have really bad hay fever. _____   **B.** You must exercise more. Try swimming.

3. I don't want to get the flu. _____   **C.** Go to the dentist and don't eat sweet desserts.

4. My tooth hurts. _____   **D.** You should gargle and wash your hands when you get home.

D. *Choose the correct word from the box that best completes the questions. Answer the questions.*

potato   much   should   many   often

1. How _____ hours do you sleep a night?   A: _____

2. How _____ junk food do you eat a week?   A: _____

3. How _____ do you clean your teeth a day?   A: _____

4. I have a bad cold. What _____ I do?   A: _____

5. My friend is a couch _____. What should he do? A: _____

MODULE 4: SELF-CHECK

A: *Write notes, words or expressions in the boxes to show what you have learned from this module.*

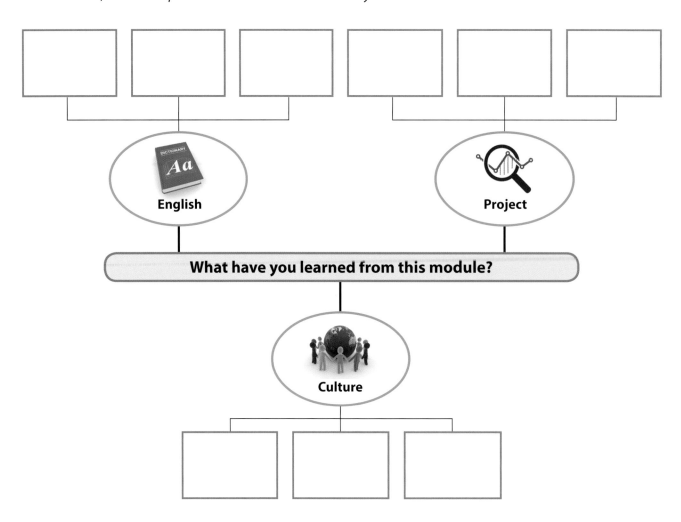

B: *Write a score (1-5)* in the boxes below to show how well you can do each part of the module. If you can't do any part well, go back to the page and practice again.*

Scan: I can scan for information about people's health (p. 55).

Speak: I can give health advice (p. 56).

Vocabulary: I can understand health vocabulary (p. 57).

Grammar: I can ask questions about health and give advice (p. 58).

Listen: I can understand conversations about health and lifestyles (p. 59).

Communicate: I can talk about my health and lifestyle (p. 60).

Read: I can read and understand people's health problems (p. 61-62).

Write: I can write a letter giving health advice (p. 65).

Project: I can find out about the health differences of my classmates (p. 66).

                 I can present data using Radar/Spider charts (p. 67).

*(1="Not at all", 2="A little", 3="OK", 4="Well", 5="Very well")

Student ID: Name:

MODULE 5: LANGUAGE REVIEW

A. *Put the verbs in the past tense.*

1. take   _____

2. fly   _____

3. drive   _____

4. come   _____

5. get   _____

6. buy   _____

7. eat   _____

8. go   _____

B. *Complete the questions below using the past tense.*

1. How _____ the hotel?

2. What _____ you buy?

3. When _____ you get back?

4. _____ the restaurants good?

5. What _____ you do yesterday?

6. How _____ the weather?

7. Where _____ your family go last weekend?

C. *Complete the answers below using the past tense. Match the answers with the questions above.*

_____ **A.** We (stay) _____ in the hotel and (relax) _____ by the pool yesterday.

_____ **B.** It (be) _____ hot and humid.

_____ **C.** We (get back) _____ last week.

_____ **D.** I (buy) _____ a really good guidebook.

_____ **E.** It (be) _____ great. The rooms (be) _____ nice and clean.

_____ **F.** They (go) _____ to the beach.

_____ **G.** No, they (be/not) _____ . We (have) _____ terrible food.

D. *Choose the correct word and complete each sentence.*

1. When you travel abroad you must have a _____ .

    a) journey   **b)** shrine   **c)** passport

2. In Japan, people often go to a _____ in the New Year holiday.

    a) temple   **b)** vacation   **c)** souvenir

3. The _____ to Europe took 12 hours. It was exhausting!

    a) flight   **b)** destination   **c)** homestay

4. I don't like big cities. I like going camping in the _____ .

    a) scenery   **b)** countryside   **c)** accommodation

E. *Choose the correct word from the box that best completes the questions. Answer the questions.*

food	souvenirs	sunny	hotel	journey

1. Did you buy any _____ ?   A: _____

2. Was the weather _____ ?   A: _____

3. What kind of _____ did you cat?   A: _____

4. How was the _____ ?   A: _____

5. Did you stay at a _____ ?   A: _____

MODULE 5: SELF-CHECK

A: *Write notes, words or expressions in the boxes to show what you have learned from this module.*

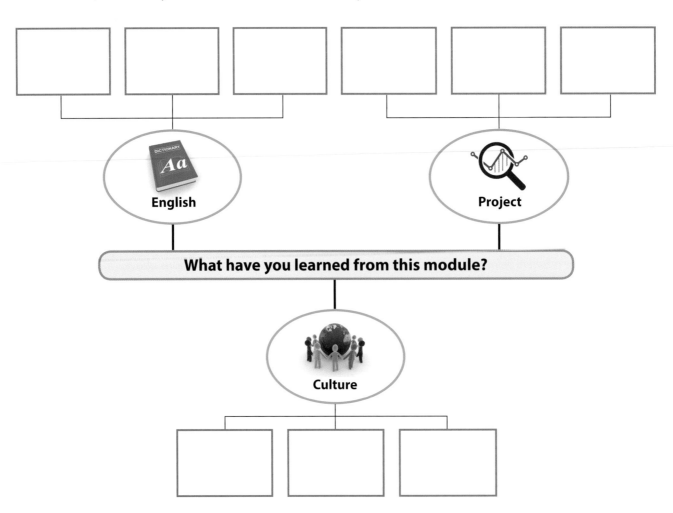

B: *Write a score (1-5)* in the boxes below to show how well you can do each part of the module. If you can't do any part well, go back to the page and practice again.*

Scan: I can scan for information about famous places (p. 71).

Speak: I can talk about my past vacations or trips (p. 72).

Vocabulary: I can understand travel vocabulary (p. 73).

Grammar: I can ask 'past' questions about travel and give answers (p. 74).

Listen: I can understand conversations about vacations (p. 75).

Communicate: I can answer questions about travel in general (p. 76).

Read: I can read and understand postcards and vacation reviews (p. 77-79).

Write: I can write about a trip I had (p. 82).

Project: I can find out about my classmates' favorite trips in Japan (p. 83).

I can present data collected from interviews (p. 83).

*(1="Not at all", 2="A little", 3="OK", 4="Well", 5="Very well")

Student ID: Name:

MODULE 6: LANGUAGE REVIEW

A. *Choose the modal verb from the box that best completes the sentences below.*

doesn't have to	mustn't	have to	couldn't
didn't have to	can	had to	

Prohibition

1. You _____ talk loudly in the library.

2. I _____ watch horror movies when I was a child. My parents didn't allow it.

Permission

3. _____ we use computers in this class?

Obligation

4. Do I _____ buy a new textbook?

5. Yesterday, I _____ attend 4 classes!

No obligation

6. He _____ work tomorrow. It's a holiday.

7. They _____ go to school yesterday because the weather was very bad.

B. *Choose the correct word and complete each sentence.*

1. You have to _____ these words to pass the test.   **a)** experience   **b)** memorize   **c)** warn

2. It is _____ to enter this room.   **a)** custom   **b)** disturb   **c)** prohibited

3. Read this sign _____.   **a)** carefully   **b)** strongly   **c)** early

4. You are not _____ to drive this car.   **a)** failed   **b)** permission   **c)** allowed

5. My high school teachers were very _____. I had to follow lots of rules.

  a) strict   **b)** public   **c)** rude

6. Please can I _____ some money from you?   **a)** pass   **b)** borrow   **c)** belong

C. *Choose the correct word from the box that best completes the questions. Answer the questions.*

course	dress	library	alcohol	driving

1. What is the _____ code at university?   A: _____

2. What is a rule for drinking _____ in Japan?   A: _____

3. What is a rule for _____ in Japan?   A: _____

4. What is a rule for this _____?   A: _____

5. What are the rules in a _____?   A: _____

MODULE 6: SELF-CHECK

A: *Write notes, words or expressions in the boxes to show what you have learned from this module.*

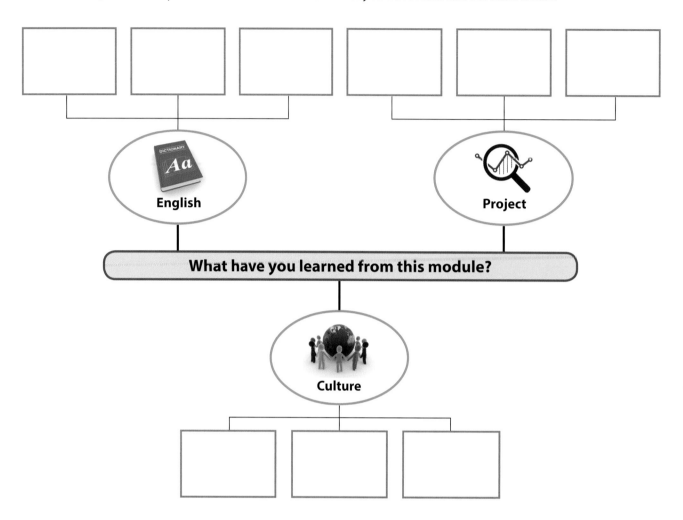

B: *Write a score (1-5)* in the boxes below to show how well you can do each part of the module. If you can't do any part well, go back to the page and practice again.*

Scan:	I can scan for information about rules (p. 87).	☐
Speak:	I can talk about rules in Japan and around the world (p. 88).	☐
Vocabulary:	I can understand rules vocabulary (p. 89).	☐
Grammar:	I can use modal verbs to discuss rules (p. 90).	☐
Listen:	I can understand conversations about rules (p. 91).	☐
Communicate:	I can talk about rules and customs around the world (p. 92-93).	☐
Read:	I can read and understand high school and university rules (p. 95).	☐
Write:	I can write about the rules at my high school and university (p. 97).	☐
Project:	I can find out important university rules from my classmates (p. 98).	☐
	I can present data using pie charts and column charts (p. 99).	☐

*(1="Not at all", 2="A little", 3="OK", 4="Well", 5="Very well")

Student ID: _____   Name: _____

MODULE 7: LANGUAGE REVIEW

A. *Change the verbs into the correct future form using "going to" or "planning to".*

1. Where (your parents / go) _____ sightseeing tomorrow?

2. My friend (visit) _____ Kyoto next spring.

3. What (you / eat) _____ for lunch?

B. *Choose (Are / Is) and change the verbs into the future form using "going to" or "planning to".*

1. _____ (they / go) _____ to Nagoya next month?

2. _____ (he / buy) _____ any souvenirs during his trip?

3. _____ (you / meet) _____ your hometown friends in the summer vacation?

C. *Arrange the words into the correct order.*

1. money / saves / if / she / she'll / on / vacation / go / year / next

_____

2. in / skiing / if / visit / you / Nagano / can / go / you / winter

_____

3. are / you / fashion / into / out / Harajuku / should / you / if / check

_____

D. *Choose the correct word and complete each sentence.*

1. My test score was _____. I made no mistakes.

  a) perfect   **b)** scenic   **c)** traditional

2. After he cleaned the room, it looked _____.

  a) pristine   **b)** nature   **c)** atmosphere

3. This view is _____. I have to take a picture.

  a) huge   **b)** modern   **c)** breathtaking

4. It's a _____ hotel. The rooms are very expensive.

  a) lively   **b)** luxurious   **c)** crowded

E. *Choose the correct word from the box to best complete the questions. Answer the questions.*

see	best	planning	vacation	festivals

1. What are you going to do in the summer _____?   A: _____

2. Are you going to _____ your high school friends soon?   A: _____

3. What are you _____ to do this weekend?   A: _____

4. Are you going to any _____ this year?   A: _____

5. What is the _____ prefecture for sightseeing?   A: _____

131

MODULE 7: SELF-CHECK

A: *Write notes, words or expressions in the boxes to show what you have learned from this module.*

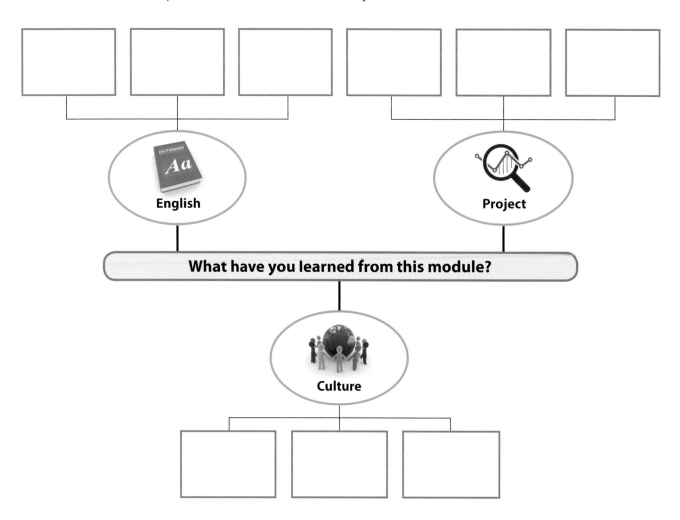

B: *Write a score (1-5)* in the boxes below to show how well you can do each part of the module. If you can't do any part well, go back to the page and practice again.*

Scan: I can scan for information about famous places in Japan (p. 103).

Speak: I can make recommendations for places to visit in Japan (p. 104).

Vocabulary: I can understand culture vocabulary (p. 105).

Grammar: I can ask questions about future plans and give recommendations (p. 106).

Listen: I can understand conversations about future plans (p. 107).

Communicate: I can answer general knowledge culture questions (p. 108-109).

Read: I can read and understand tourism advertisements (p. 111).

Write: I can write an advertisement about a place I know well (p. 113).

Project: I can find out Japan's tourist attractions from my classmates (p. 114).

                 I can present data collected from interviews. (p. 115).

*(1="Not at all", 2="A little", 3="OK", 4="Well", 5="Very well")

Student ID: _____   Name: _____